How to be a Fantastic Writer

A handbook for writers of commercial fiction

How to be a Fantastic Writer

A handbook for writers of commercial fiction

Penny Grubb & Danuta Reah

First published June 2012 by
Fantastic Books Publishing as *The Writers' Toolkit*

This edition published September 2017
by Fantastic Books Publishing

Cover design by Gabi

ISBN (ebook): 978-1-912053-54-4
ISBN (2nd Edition paperback): 978-1-912053- 55-1

Contents

Introduction

....

What this book is about

The purpose of this book is to provide toolkits and techniques that will help writers of commercial fiction to structure, create and edit their novels. This book does not aim to turn you into a great writer or editor, but if you are capable of great writing and editing this book will help you to produce great commercial fiction.

We look at the basic components of commercial fiction and how they fit together. We have studied the work of previous scholars of commercial fiction from Charles Dickens to Stephen King; from J D Salinger to James Herriot. We use practical examples taken from a wide range that includes Kurt Vonnegut, Joss Whedon and Ridley Scott. We have studied academic writings on structure and form of the novel, and we have looked at the structure and techniques of various commercial fiction authors including ourselves. A list of our sources is included in the bibliography.

We believe that commercial fiction has a generic structure underlying it. In setting out the detail of this, we hope to give commercial fiction authors a better understanding of the way they structure their work.

The underlying concepts for this work have been based around how readers read and what they expect and want from a work of commercial fiction.

Do we believe that works of commercial fiction can be written by rote? No, we don't, but we believe that an analysis of the elements of the different parts of the narrative tale is useful e.g. to get started on an awkward scene, to decide what should and shouldn't be included; to identify why a scene isn't dramatic enough, isn't emotional enough, isn't reflective enough, or just plain doesn't work. This is not an attempt to provide a write-by-numbers technique and you should be clear that this book does not substitute for work on plotting, characterisation and background research. However, using the toolkits can help writers to understand structures such as flashback, time-jumps, point-of-view and descriptive prose, and how different approaches can affect the pace and tension of a scene.

We believe in these techniques and structures and we use them in our own writing. We hope they will be useful to anyone who writes commercial fiction. As with all techniques, it is important to discover what works for you. In using this book you might find the overview more useful than the detailed toolkits or vice versa. New writers might find the techniques useful to help plot their novels. Experienced writers for whom plotting is not a problem might instead use the techniques as repair kits for problematic sections in their manuscripts.

When we teach these techniques in workshops, we structure the classes so that the students can work on their own manuscripts along the way. Our workshops are based around the structure of the novel – the start, the middle and the end. We teach these either as one-off sessions on particular topics or as a series of sessions working through the whole of the novel.

We begin with a high-level overview of a work of commercial fiction. Then we look in detail at each of these elements:

- how to write a compelling start,
- how to build the peaks and troughs of the story as it unfolds,
- how to round off the story into a satisfying finish.

Our aim in writing this book is to share the toolkits and techniques that have helped us and that we hope will help you with your writing.

CHAPTER ONE

What draws a reader to a book

....

This chapter will look at
- the overall structure of a work of commercial fiction
- what makes a reader pick up a book – that's a reader looking for a good read and also an agent or editor looking for a client
- what keeps a reader reading
- how to pitch your work in no more than two sentences
- techniques for establishing a character.

The overall structure

It's pretty simple. The book has a cover, the cover has a blurb. Inside the book, the story has a beginning, a middle and an end.

Books are often sold on their covers. Traditionally that's something over which the author has little control. However, with the rise in self-publishing this is already beginning to change and will be something that self-published authors need to learn about. However, cover design is not an area we look at.

Traditionally, authors also have little control over the blurb, but we are going to look at the blurb because it's a very useful structure for pitching a book. Before we get into the detail, let's look at things from the readers' perspective.

In a work of commercial fiction the reader is looking for a

good read. They pick up the book and start to read. Why? What is it that attracts them? It might be that this is a book by one of their favourite authors, but for the moment let's suppose not. Other than the cover the first thing a reader looks at is usually the blurb. If that takes their interest, they'll turn to the first page and read a few lines.

Of course, different people assess books in different ways. Some readers never read blurbs, some deliberately go straight to the middle of the book or to the end. However we are dealing with what happens in most cases, and the usual route is cover to blurb to first page.

The average reader assesses a book in just a few seconds. So if they are to be tempted into going further then something must pique their curiosity enough to read on.

Once a reader has started to read, it is the job of the writer to hold them, sentence by sentence, paragraph by paragraph until they are hooked. The reader is hooked at the point they engage with the characters and the story; the point where they actively want to dive into the whole book.

The opening sequence has a special role. This is the part of the book where the reader has not yet committed to the story. It is the job of the opening sequence to draw the reader in, bit by bit until they are sufficiently engaged that they make the decision to commit to the book. The component parts of this opening sequence and how they work together are the subject of the chapter *Creating a compelling opening*.

Once the story has gone beyond the opening sequence it moves through the book in a series of peaks and troughs. The peaks are moments of rising tension, climactic moments, nail-biting cliff hangers. In the troughs the tension is released, the characters (and the readers) relax and take stock. The usual structure will be that the rising-tension scenes increase as the book progresses and those moments of sitting back and taking stock become shorter.

Rising-tension scenes end on a moment of high drama which can be an action-packed point of sudden disaster or something more subtle; a character teetering at the brink of a cliff or an apparently innocent remark spawning the realisation of impending calamity. Because of the cliff hanger nature of the rising-tension scene, chapters will often end on these page-turner moments. Similarly, chapters will often begin with a scene that releases tension. Don't mistake releasing tension for lack of drama. Written properly, these scenes will have the readers on the edges of their seats every bit as much as the rest.

The chapters dealing with these constructs are *The scene that builds tension* and *The scene that releases tension*. These chapters will break down each type of scene into its component parts and show you how to put them together.

A work of commercial fiction ultimately reaches a climax and a resolution. The readers' journey through the book has ended. If it has been a good and well-written book, they will sit back satisfied they have had a good read, happy with where the story ended and hopefully thirsting for more from the same author. Bringing a work of commercial fiction to a satisfying conclusion also requires particular components and structures whether it is to be a happy ending or not. The chapter dealing with this in detail is *Bringing the story to a satisfying end*.

Always be aware that having all the right components does not in itself create a good or well-written novel any more than having a pile of bricks and a cement mixer means you can build a house, but with the right tools you give yourself the best chance. And to help you on your way, each of the chapters contains a section that goes into more detail on specific techniques showing how you can weave these into your own writing to bring your story to life.

In order to sell your work to a reader, an agent or a publisher you need a compelling blurb or pitch that makes your book stand out from the pack. The first of the detailed toolkit sections shows you how to do this. Bear in mind that we are working through the book following the readers' journey so that we can focus on what makes a gripping tale from their point of view. Creating the pitch or the blurb is not step one for the writer. Before you can do this exercise, you need to know your book. You might already have written it; you might have planned it but not yet written a word of the manuscript itself; you might simply be working from an idea. As well as providing a useful pitch, this exercise will help you focus on the bigger picture.

How to create a compelling pitch

A blurb or pitch can be a key tool for drawing in a reader at least as far as the first page. Traditionally, the writer doesn't write the blurb; that's a job for the publisher. However, a good blurb is nothing more than a concise pitch for the book. It's just what you need when pitching to a busy agent or editor. So even if your blurb might not be used on the finished product it's worth learning how to create it.

A concise two-sentence pitch

In every work of commercial fiction it is possible to find five elements that you can use to create a blurb or a pitch.

The first three are:

1. A character: Who is your main character?
2. An objective: What is his or her objective?
3. A situation: Your main character is in a sticky situation at some point in the story. What is it?

There are likely to be several answers to these questions. Usually in commercial fiction there is a clearly identifiable main character, but there may be more than one. The character you choose may have different objectives at different points in the story. Note however that the main character usually has an over-arching objective. Likewise your character will go through several sticky situations as the story progresses. For this exercise you should use an important objective and a sticky situation that threatens its success.

The last two elements are:

4. An opponent: Someone or something stands in your character's way. Who or what?
5. A disaster: Your character will be faced with disastrous consequences as a result of the opponent. What is the disaster?

Again, there may be multiple examples. At different times your character will meet different types of opposition and will face different consequences. Which do you choose? You experiment and see which gives you the most effective pitch.

Here's how:
- Take the first three elements and turn them into a single statement.
- Take the last two and turn them into a question.

For example:
1. Character – Jack Smith.
2. Objective – to climb Mount Everest.
3. Situation – the summit is 20 minutes away.
4. Opponent – the clock. He has to turn back in 25 minutes or he won't be able to get back down.
5. Disaster – another climber asks for his help.

Putting the first three elements into a single statement:

Jack Smith has sold everything to fund his attempt to climb Everest and he stands within sight of his goal.

Making a question of the last two elements:

Will he lose this only chance to fulfil a lifetime ambition when a stranger calls for help?

Putting these together gives you a concise pitch that encapsulates the key points of the story.

Jack Smith has sold everything to fund his attempt to climb Everest and he stands within sight of his goal. Will he lose his only chance to fulfil a lifetime ambition when a stranger calls for help?

Worked examples from Strangers, Waiting for Gordo and Like False Money

Strangers

1. Character – Roisin.
2. Objective – to find out her husband's secret.
3. Situation – after an impulsive marriage to Joe, Roisin is now an ex-pat in Saudi Arabia, and is beginning to realise her husband is not all he seemed.
4. Opponent – a system that keeps women like Roisin closeted and restricted.
5. Disaster – a precipitating event means things will move more quickly than Roisin can understand.

Roisin wants to make a success of her new marriage and her life in a new country, but she is beginning to realise her husband, Joe, has reasons for returning to Saudi Arabia that he has not told her. Will she find out what is going on before a culture she does not understand destroys them both?

Waiting for Gordo

1. Character – Miranda.
2. Objective – to have a relaxing holiday with a small party of friends on a tiny island in the Indian Ocean.

3. Situation – she begins to feel that she is being watched.
4. Opponent – an unknown presence on the island.
5. Disaster – two of their party disappear.

When Miranda and her husband, Jim, arrive on the idyllic island with a small party of friends, she looks forward to a relaxing holiday. When two of the group fail to appear at supper, Miranda knows they are not just "late as usual", but can she convey her growing unease to the rest of the party before disaster overtakes them all?

Like False Money
1. Character – Annie Raymond.
2. Objective – to be taken seriously as a private investigator.
3. Situation – thrown in at the deep end in her first job.
4. Opponent – a young schoolgirl.
5. Disaster – she is accused of malpractice.

Annie Raymond, desperate to be taken seriously as a private investigator, finds herself in an impossible job with a boss who hasn't a clue who she is. Will her career be over before it starts when a schoolgirl accuses her of unprofessional conduct?

In the original pitch to the publisher, this was contracted even further to:

Can fledgling PI Annie Raymond cut it on her own when faced with a job she can't do, a boss who hasn't a clue who she is, and a schoolgirl ready to blacken her name to save her own skin?

This was the pitch used to sell the book. The publisher took the essence of it into the final blurb.

These short pitches don't tell the story of the book in any detail. They are more of a snapshot than an outline. The important thing is that they introduce the main character, say something about his or her motivation and then they raise a question, hopefully leaving the reader curious enough to read on.

Toolkit for the pitch

Your turn now. Answer the questions below for the main character in your own novel. Once you have the elements turn them into a statement and a question and try to create a pitch.

Situation:	
Character:	
Objective:	
Turn these three elements into one sentence: a statement:	
Opponent:	
Disaster:	
Turn these two elements into one sentence: a question:	

In order to remain true to the book you should always use the story's main character and one of their major objectives, but you can experiment with different types of opposition and a variety of situations where your character faces various potential consequences.

Advanced techniques

Establishing your fictional world and characters

Before you can write a book that will grip a reader, you need to know what it's about; you need to know its fictional world and its characters, and you need to know them well. You also need your readers to identify the important aspects of this world: What kind of place is this? What kind of person is this?

You could just spell it all out but this would make for a long and dull piece of writing.

Further techniques for developing characters and establishing a sense of place are looked at later in this book, but here are some of the techniques a writer can use to establish a character:

In each of these short extracts, a character looks at herself in the mirror. What effect does this same action have in each extract? What actions or mannerisms does the character have, and what effect does this create?

1. She could see herself in the mirror behind him, and enjoyed the view for a few seconds before she turned her attention back to what he was saying. 'That's so interesting,' she murmured.

2. She straightened her shoulders and glanced sideways at

herself in the mirror. 'OK.' She smiled as the secretary ushered her into the room.

3. She glanced in the mirror and pushed her hair back from her face. People were moving round the room now, greeting each other, chatting, circulating. She smiled, and glanced in the mirror again, shaking her hair forward. Why did lipstick never stay on for more than a few minutes? 'Hi,' she greeted a woman coming past with a tray in her hand. The woman gave her an odd look and proffered the tray. 'White wine, ma'am?'

Think about what you have learnt about the woman in these short extracts. How do you feel towards her? In each case there is something there to push you towards an impression of the woman's character, and it is different each time.

In extract 1, the impression is languid and relaxed; a woman more interested in how she looks than in listening to her companion. Extract 2 shows us a woman girding herself for action, less interested in what she sees in the mirror than in what awaits in the room she enters. Extract 3 shows a woman who is uncomfortable, unconfident in both herself and the event she is attending. Yet none of this is stated explicitly.

Remember also that these extracts are seen through the eyes of the unnamed woman. They are *her* impressions and not necessarily how anyone else would see things. For example, in J D Salinger's *The Catcher in the Rye*, Holden Caulfield, the main character through whose eyes we see the story, tells us *I'm this kind of person, I'm that kind of person* – but, this is not how Holden is at all. It is only how he sees himself.

Consider this extract from *Waiting for Gordo*. This is Miranda and Jim's first night in a holiday villa on a tropical island:

> *Perhaps she should have had a beer or two and then she might have been sleeping as soundly as Jim, Miranda regretted, as she tiptoed out of the bathroom, keeping a wary eye on the large golden cockroach, which seemed to be watching her just as intently from behind the mirror. Perhaps there was a whole gang of cockroaches inside their little hide – all watching her through binoculars? 'It's a Red-Haired Miranda!' they'd be exclaiming geekishly. 'Its colours are fading and it's past its prime', as they ticked her off in their People-Spotting albums.*

What can you say from this about Miranda? What is your impression of her relationship with her husband, Jim? What is her mood? What age would you guess her to be?

The messages are that she is considerate of Jim, she tiptoes so as not to wake him; she is 'past her prime'; Jim has had 'a beer or two', but it is mentioned in passing without any implication of excessive drinking; Miranda herself has not had a beer but implies that she might on another occasion; she makes light of the cockroach, despite keeping a 'wary eye' on it; she has red hair.

Miranda is focused mainly on the cockroach, as would many of us be on a late night trip to the bathroom on a tropical island. This allows the reader to empathise and to absorb the rest of the information without any particular feeling that it is being doled out for their benefit. The author also uses the image of the 'watching' cockroach as she builds a far more sinister ambience as the holiday progresses. It's a clever device that starts out lightheartedly with the 'People-Spotting' insects and escalates, giving the reader a growing sense of something nasty just out of sight.

The right choice of words

A simple choice of words can tell the reader a lot about a character, and about the world that character inhabits. Brett Easton Ellis's *American Psycho* is peppered with brand names all through the book. In the world of the main character, Patrick Bateman, owning the right brand, and going to the right places is fundamentally important to the world he inhabits. Just by the use of these words, Ellis creates a world of empty, driving materialism.

Simple choices can speak volumes. What breakfast cereal does your character eat? Cornflakes? Alpen? Muesli? What effect does each choice create?

Think about a female character you are planning for your narrative. What does she drink: beer, wine, spirits ...? If beer, does she prefer bitter or mild, does she drink pints or half pints? If she prefers wine, is it red or white? Is it fine wine or a supermarket offer? Does she drink a glass with a meal or a bottle by herself? How about whisky, gin or vodka? What brand?

Now consider one of your male characters. Does he like beer? Is his preference bitter, lager or some specialist bottled brand? What about his taste in wine? What type of spirits does he like?

Each choice you make tells you something about your character.

This extract is from a short story, *No Flies on Frank*.

> Cynthia studied the envelope. 'Cowlishaw and Thring,' she said. 'Solicitors.' She fixed her husband with a suspicious gaze. 'What have you been up to now, Harry?'
> Harry concentrated on his cornflakes.

Think about the impression this gives you of Harry. Then consider what difference it would make if Harry was eating muesli, or a croissant, or black pudding.

The following passage offers a series of options. Experiment with the options given and consider the effects you create. Think also about what other choices you might include to create different effects.

> The barman/barmaid/girl behind the bar saw Avery come in and reached for a pint pot/glass/shot glass/tumbler. He/she reached for the tap/bottle and Avery watched the dark/pale/yellowish/ruby red liquid swirl round the bottom of the glass/pint pot/tumbler and gleam in the dim light from the dirty bulb/shaded lamp.

Consider how different choices will give you different impressions of the characters and the setting. Is Avery a man or a woman? Clearly Avery and the person behind the bar know each other. What is the relationship? Who holds the power? These exercises where you play around with your characters' preferences are useful in reinforcing the character traits in your own mind and will provide you with some valuable snippets to colour your prose.

Should you plan your novel or not?

Despite many texts telling you that you must plan if you want to avoid disaster, there really is no rule. Some writers plan in such detail they have a book-length plan before they start to write. Others just go by the seat of their pants. The majority probably fall somewhere in between the extremes. When you're starting out, it makes sense to try different techniques, but never feel obliged to go one route with your writing just because it worked for someone else. In the end it comes down to what works for you.

We have now persuaded the reader to take the book off the shelf, read the blurb and turn to the first page. The next thing is to create a compelling opening.

CHAPTER TWO

Creating a compelling opening

This chapter will look at
- the opening sequence of the book and what it aims to do
- the importance of creating a compelling first paragraph
- where and why the opening sequence begins and ends
- techniques for piquing the readers' curiosity in the opening paragraphs.

The opening sequence in overview

Always remember who the reader is. Don't think of your reader as someone thirsting to read your prose; think of your reader as someone who has picked your book at random from the bookshop display or the agent's slush pile. Let us assume this reader has been attracted by the blurb or pitch and has made it as far as the first sentence. At this point, the reader is not engaged with the story or the characters; they don't care what's going to happen in the end.

How do you keep them reading further?

The trick is to make them care what happens in the very next sentence, the very next paragraph ... draw them in bit by bit until they buy into the story and make the decision to carry on through the book.

When something out of the ordinary happens, people stop

and look. Think about a sudden shout in a busy street. Heads turn as people try to see what is happening. If it is someone shouting to stop a child wandering into a line of fast-moving traffic, you will be momentarily shocked, transfixed, willing someone to get there in time, and unable to tear your gaze from the drama until you see it resolved. But then suppose someone else from the crowd, a stranger, comes up to you and begins to tell you their life story. At this point you will back away with a murmured excuse and make your escape. Their life story might be very interesting, but you don't know this person, you have no reason to invest your time in stopping in the street long enough to hear the whole convoluted tale. Of course it might be quite different if you got to know this person and the story began to leak out bit by bit. You would get to the point of actively wanting to know more. But for that random encounter in the street, the sudden shout will take your attention for a moment; the promise of the detailed life story will simply make you run.

Your opening needs to be the sudden shout and not the promise of a long detailed story. Reel in your reader bit by bit until they want to know more. This is how to grab the random reader. How does this work in practical terms?

A point of change

Begin your story at a point of change. Promise just enough that the reader stops and looks at the next sentence and then the next and so on until, if you get it right, the reader commits to the book i.e. they want to know about the characters and the story.

There are certain things that should not appear in the opening sequence – these are the things that the reader does not care about until they have committed to the book. For example, your characters might have done some fascinating things in the past that are of vital importance to the plot, but don't explain them in the opening sequence. Once the reader has committed to the book they will be every bit as interested as you in the characters' backgrounds and psychologies but at the start, they couldn't care less.

There are some things that should explicitly appear in the opening sequence. These are to do with giving the readers anchors so that they don't misread the story. If you don't provide anchors, the readers will make up their own and this can cause problems. More on this in the following sections.

If you do a good job of the opening sequence, there will come a point where the reader buys in; they will commit to the book and want to read on. At this point, they no longer need, or indeed want, to be tempted along bit by bit. They are ready to dive into the complexities of the tale. Once the readers are at this point, the structure must change. A book will become irritating if it carries on trying to pull in the readers bit by bit after they have decided they want the big picture. Thus the opening sequence needs to come to a specific end. Later sections in this chapter will show how this works and how to do it.

How long is the opening sequence?

An opening sequence is rarely longer than a chapter. If the reader hasn't bought into the book by the end of the first chapter, they probably aren't going to buy in at all. But equally, a book can raise such an intriguing question that the reader will buy into it almost at once, making the opening sequence no more than a few paragraphs. Whenever you find a book that really grips you, analyse the opening sequence and identify what drew you in.

Always bear in mind we are talking about commercial fiction and books that provide a good read without the reader having to do too much work themselves. There are many books that call for the reader to work hard to get themselves involved; books that demand reader commitment, that are not immediately accessible. And many of these are incredibly good reads for those who invest the time to get into them. But what we are looking at here is commercial fiction specifically designed to be an easy and gripping read.

How to construct the opening sequence

The start point

It's easy to say start at a point of change, but it isn't actually a point, it's a range. The range stretches from before the change, right through the change to after the change. Where exactly do you start? There's no single right answer, each book is different. There can be several right answers and each point of the range has its pitfalls.

Starting before the change means you are promising imminent change with consequences that the reader will be curious to see. But beware starting too early. The reader who is not yet engaged in the book will not read on very far waiting for something to happen.

Starting as the change happens can provide a very dynamic and dramatic opening. The potential problem is that because you must stay right within the action, it can be hard to convey details of who, what and when. This can leave the reader in limbo knowing for instance that they're with a character in the middle of a sudden attack but having no anchors to know if it's a man or woman, child or adult, night or day etc. This sort of confusion can pull the reader out of the text.

Starting after the change means you can dive right into some very interesting consequences, but the change that led up to them will have to be explained at some point. Beware falling into the trap of too much explanation too early because until the reader has committed to the book, they won't be interested in what went before.

In *Buried Deep*, the story starts just moments before the private investigator Annie realises that her routine surveillance is anything but.

In *Tiger Blood*, the story starts mid change. Detective Superintendent Webber has been pulled away from what he considers the urgent work of the day and set to look at an old crime. The opening sequence pitches the reader into the middle of his confusion as he tries to work out what his boss is playing at.

In *Night Angels*, the story starts after the change. Gemma has already noted the car pulling out behind her. The reader is pitched right into the consequences of the dawning realisation that it is not following her by chance.

You will find valid start points all along the range but take the time to think about before, during or after. And be aware of the pitfalls of each choice.

The opening sentences

The opening sentences of your book are gold dust. Their importance cannot be overstated. If the reader is bored or simply not interested by the first sentence they will probably close the book and go on to something else. You must pique the readers' curiosity from the start. Ways to do this include:

1. Raising a question in the readers' minds.

This should be an immediate question, one where it looks as though there will be a quick answer. This is not the place to raise a big question that will not be answered until the end of the book. The aim is to make the reader curious enough that they decide to read the rest of the paragraph.

> It was a Thursday in December, the night that Debbie saw the killer.

This is the opening sentence from *Only Darkness*. This looks like a big question on the face of it. Who is the killer? Who has been killed? But if you think about your reaction to something like this, it isn't immediately to know all about the killer and the killing, it's just to know the circumstances in which Debbie saw the killer. We don't know if the killer saw Debbie or even if Debbie knows what she saw, but the words hold the promise that we will see this intriguing encounter soon if we read on.

2. Opening with something unexpected.

The unexpected tends to grab our attention even if only temporarily. Remember that 'sudden shout in the street'.

> *Ted had just relaxed back into the cushions, pack of chips balanced in his lap, TV remote poised to play the film, when a sudden blaze of light jerked him upright and a tremendous crash sounded from behind.*

This isn't much as it stands. It tells us Ted was getting ready to relax and not expecting interruption. A crash from behind could be something as mundane as a badly balanced stack of plates falling to the floor. But there's that blaze of light too. Plates don't fall in a blaze of light. Ted will surely leap to his feet and turn round to see what's happening, and the random reader might just decide to stick around long enough to turn with him and find out what it was.

3. Conveying an air of menace.

This is an opening often used in film. Everything is very normal and ordinary, but we have a sense of something terribly wrong that we can't yet quite see. A chilling sense of menace behind a sequence where everything appears to be normal can make for a gripping opening. In a film, menace can be conveyed by background music or camera angles, but how do you do this on the page?

The trick is to use an inordinate amount of detail to the point that the reader knows that something must be very wrong behind it. There is a hint of this in the opening to *Only Darkness*.

Debbie's home time routine is ordinary, but we as readers are aware of impending menace.

The following is the first paragraph from *Where There's Smoke*. It holds a lot of detail but at the same time bristles with the characters' hidden agendas and makes clear that this is the 'last short stretch' which says to the reader: Read on and see where the boat will land.

> *Waves slapped against the low sides of the boat, salt water splashing in the darkness, pinpricks on Vitoria's skin. The night air cut across her, emphasizing her sense of isolation, but she felt no fear, just an exhilaration she held tight to herself. Her pilot for this last short stretch, cut the motor, swivelled the tiny outboard free of the water and pulled a pair of oars from the floor of the craft. As he did so he glanced at her as though wondering if the move would alarm her. Maybe it would have if she hadn't understood every word of the quick fire exchanges before she'd been pushed out into his care. As they'd helped her make the precarious step into the smaller boat over the churning oily blackness between the two craft, she had pretended to need their exaggerated sign language.*

The following is the first paragraph from *Till They Dropped*. It is busy with detail; the plaza, the humming booth churning out ice-cream sodas, the taped splashing of the fountain, but there is a sense of menace behind it. What was the rustling that she heard? What is the dead area where she hadn't been able to find water? Why is the splashing fountain taped? There is the promise of having at least one of these questions unravelled within a paragraph or so.

Emily had been sitting in the plaza for some time, before she heard the rustling. She had been so thirsty after those days in the dead area that all she had thought of was water. The humming booth had churned out ice-cream sodas which she greedily gulped down. She listened – ice-cream soda hands frozen in mid-air – but there was no further sound, only the taped splashing of the fountain.

Be aware however that an inordinate amount of detail on its own is simply that – a lot of detail. What is it that signals the air of menace that in a film would be shown in the background music or the camera angle that zooms up close to a character as though someone is behind them? These are techniques that modern novelists have borrowed from the world of film. For more detail, see the *Advanced Techniques* sections of this and later chapters.

4. Giving a simple indication that something is out of the ordinary.

This is similar to the way someone's attention is caught by a random comment overheard on a train. It piques the curiosity just enough to make the reader or the listener want to know more. The element that is out of the ordinary can be very small and very subtle; it is the fact of it being out of the ordinary for a particular character that raises the question in the readers' minds as to why.

Instead of driving across the intersection, Rod paused, glanced briefly over his shoulder and then flicked on his right-hand indicator.

It is nothing much, but it's clearly out of the ordinary. Whoever Rod is, he would usually go straight on, but he didn't. He decided to turn right. Furthermore, he did it after a brief glance round. That makes something surreptitious about it. It raises the question Why?

One sultry evening in July a young man emerged from the small furnished room he occupied in a large five-storied house in Sennoy Lane and turned slowly, with an air of indecision towards the Kalininsky Bridge.

This is the opening sentence from *Crime and Punishment*. It is the 'slowly' and the 'air of indecision' that signal this as something out of the normal run of things.

5. Surprising the reader

Use the readers' own preconceptions to set up a particular expectation or simply have something downright odd happen. For example, refer to a character taking the lid off something that doesn't have a lid.

Mary lifted the lid and looked inside the tree.

Or describe a particular type of person and then make that person act completely outside their stereotype e.g. a small fluffy-haired old lady who sits down to a cup of tea and then gift-wraps a sex-toy.

This type of opening grabs the readers' attention because it surprises them. With luck they will want to read on just to make sense of the initial set up.

What to include

When readers begin to read they will make their own assumptions. In particular at the start of the book they will make assumptions about where, what and who.

For example, if you don't indicate clearly that the action is taking place on a windy beach, the readers might paint pictures in their heads of a dark enclosed cellar. Similarly if you don't give some indication of the age of the characters in the opening sequence the readers will make their own assumptions. This can cause problems when the reader paints a very different picture from the one that you intend. Your characters might be in their 50s but if the readers have assumed them to be 20-somethings they will be jolted out of the story at the point they realise their mistake. The pictures they build in their minds are vital to building their commitment to the book. If these are suddenly shown to be entirely wrong you risk losing them because they must rewind and start again, seeing all the action with a different set of characters. That is a lot to ask of a random reader who is not yet engaged with the story.

Bear this in mind when writing the opening sequence and make sure that you include enough clues and description to give an accurate enough picture of where the action is taking place, the context and the characters, particularly their ages. You don't need to say exactly how old everybody is but you should give some clue.

What to avoid

The big aim of the opening sequence is to grab the readers by the techniques already outlined and then to hold on to them by keeping them close to the action and rousing their curiosity about what is happening. There are various things that will pull the reader out of the story. These are the things you should avoid.

- Do not introduce too many characters. Your book might have a large cast and all the characters might be vital to the story, but don't throw too many of them at the readers right at the start. Remember they don't know anything about this book, they really couldn't care less about what happens to whom, and if you confuse them with a large cast you will put them off.
- The opening sequence will be written from a particular viewpoint. You are taking the readers along with you from within the mind of one of the characters. Assuming you do a good job, you will be gradually engaging them in the views and viewpoints of a particular character. If you switch to another viewpoint within the opening sequence you are essentially asking them to start again and re-engage with the book from a different character's point of view. That is a big ask before a reader is properly engaged in a book. Stick with a single viewpoint for the opening sequence.
- Your characters probably have a fascinating history and have done some amazing things in the past, but beware of describing this in the opening sequence. At the point where you are drawing the readers in bit by bit all you can rely on is their curiosity, their desire to know what happens next. They will not engage with what has already happened. Once the readers have bought into the book they will be only too pleased to hear all the detail

of those fascinating events that happened in the past – in so far as they are relevant to the story of course – but not right at the start. Avoid back story in the opening sequence.

- Never mislead the readers. If your viewpoint character is thinking or feeling something, the readers need to know about it. They are effectively behind that character's eyes and in that character's head. They will feel cheated if it turns out that they were denied this knowledge. If you don't want to reveal what a particular character is thinking and feeling, then don't make him/her the viewpoint character.

- Very often the events that happened in the past, by which I mean before the point where the book starts, are key events in the story. There will be times in the book where you might go back and re-live the sequences in flashback so that the readers go through the experience with the characters. That's fine, but not in the opening sequence. Remember that before the readers are engaged with the book, they couldn't care less what went before. You are only hooking them in with their curiosity as to what happens next. So no matter how dramatic or exciting a particular event is, do not tell it in flashback at the start of the book. If such a sequence has to go at the start of the book, then maybe that is where the book needs to start in real time.

Rules or guidelines

Should you, as a writer of commercial fiction, take these to be 'rules', and stick like glue to the toolkits? No, of course not, but recognising the elements gives you a far better chance of being effective when you deviate from the structure.

Only Darkness, whose opening line was used as an example above, is itself a useful example of someone not sticking rigidly to the 'rules'. There is a taste of back story in the opening sequence as Debbie gets ready to leave and head for her train, but the question is intriguing enough to hold the reader because we know that this scene is leading up to Debbie seeing the killer.

And there is a change of viewpoint. The opening sentence is omniscient. Apart from that, the sequence is all from Debbie's point of view. It works because that initial omniscient viewpoint is short and it hits the reader hard and fast. And it isn't repeated. Because of the opening, when the figure at the station appears briefly, we know what she's seen, but she doesn't. Without that opening sentence, would a random reader read on?

The opening chapter leading up to Debbie's encounter at the station, is short. If there had been too much detail about Debbie's background, it could lose the reader. And if that omniscient voice had made another appearance that too could have pulled the reader right out of the story.

In her novel, *The Group*, Mary McCarthy tells the story of a group of young women friends growing up in 1930s America. The first and final chapters are told via an omniscient narrator, with an occasional move into the minds of the different women, but each chapter is written entirely in the 'voice' of the character central to that episode. For a writer who is interested in the ways point of view can be used, McCarthy offers a masterclass (as well as an extremely engaging novel).

Bringing the opening sequence to an end

Once you've captured the readers and they have become engaged enough to want to read the book, you have to stop the business of reeling them in bit by bit. If you don't, you risk losing them because they will become irritated. *Enough with the intriguing tasters. I want the real story!*

How do you know you've reached the right point? You make your own judgment as to when you feel that a reader who is going to be intrigued will have reached the point of committing to the story. You can't reel everyone in, but you judge the point of commitment for someone who will be drawn to your book.

What happens at the point where the opening sequence ends and the story proper begins? How does the narrative signal that this has happened? In essence, you reward the reader for committing to the book by showing that a key character has also made a commitment. You show this by having your character make a decision. Not just any decision. It must signal a significant commitment on their part.

Worked example from *Syrup Trap City*

The start point

Q: What is the change?
A: Maximillian Corder's deviation from his routine, not just to have a drink on the way to his meeting but because he 'likes to see people squirm'.

Q: What are the potential consequences?
A: He has the power to close the restaurant. The reader (being inside his head) knows he has no intention of doing so, but those who would be affected don't have this reassurance.

Q: Who will be affected by these?
A: The restaurant manager and staff, one of whom turns out to be the private investigator, Annie.

Q: Does the book start before, during or after the change?
A: Before.

The opening sequence

Q: What technique is used to pique the curiosity?
A: Raise a question / the unexpected / something out of the ordinary. The initial question is who is Corder and who will squirm at his unexpected presence? The arrival of the off-duty detective and Corder's reaction are unexpected. At the start, the reader is ahead of the restaurant staff by virtue of being inside Corder's head. They know Corder won't close the place. The arrival of the detective turns the tables on Corder but he sees enough to know he wasn't the only one to recognise the man. And there is a mini-reward for readers of this series of books who will recognise the name, Annie, when Corder overhears it, and will find themselves a step ahead of the viewpoint character as they will know that Annie is a private detective and he doesn't.

Q: Where is the opening sequence set?
A: In the restaurant in the centre of Hull.

Q: Who is the main character in the opening sequence and how will you convey the necessary information e.g. age?
A: Corder. Information conveyed using his arrogance and thoughts about how he will intimidate the staff.

Q: What is happening and where? How will you convey this?
A: A restaurant building towards a busy lunchtime. Use the tensions of Corder's unexpected arrival, plus his deliberately sitting at a reserved table for six, so we can see the hubbub and angst of others through his eyes as he relaxes.

How is the opening scene brought to a close?

Q: What is the decision / commitment made?
A: The decision to check out the new assistant manager, but also to leave before the detective notices him.

Q: Which character makes this decision / commitment?
A: Corder.

Worked example from *The Doll Makers*

The start point

Q: What is the change?
A: The devastation that will occur when Annie talks to her father to tell him what she's done.

Q: What are the potential consequences?
A: She will have completely disrupted his life, just as he is winding down to retirement.

Q: Who will be affected by these?
A: Annie, her father and her aunt.

Q: Does the book start before, during or after the change?
A: Before.

The opening sequence

Q: What technique is used to pique the curiosity?
A: Raise a question / normal routine but something wrong. This in an example of raising a question but having the question change as the scene develops. The initial question is what words? Then what is she going to say to her father? Also an element of normal routine but something wrong – in this case everything is normal for Annie's father but about to go wrong.

Note that what keeps the reader reading is not the major disruption that Annie might cause to her father (the reader doesn't care about either of them at this stage), it's that all too human fascination with witnessing the drama; being the fly on the wall when she has to have the awkward conversation with him.

Q: Where is the opening sequence set?
A: On the drive to Scotland, across on the ferry and to Annie's childhood home.

Q: Who is the main character in the opening sequence and how will you convey the necessary information e.g. age?
A: Annie. Information conveyed using her worries about how she will appear to her father. She contrasts her 8-year-old self to her present 28-year-old self.

Q: What is happening and where? How will you convey this?
A: Long hot drive. Annie's worry escalates. Use the tensions and discomforts of a long drive in an unreliable car, then contrast with Glasgow early morning and the loch side on a summer day.

How is the opening scene brought to a close?

Q: What is the decision / commitment made?
A: The decision to deal with the unrevealed something on her own

Q: Which character makes this decision / commitment?
A: Annie.

Worked example from *The Last Room*

The start point

Q: What is the change?
A: A young woman is attacked in a village in Cote d'Ivoire. She has to protect her children.

Q: What are the potential consequences?
A: As a result of the attack, she flees the country with her husband and children and is now an asylum seeker in Manchester.

Q: Who will be affected by these?
A: The woman, Nadifa, and ultimately, forensic linguist Ania and her father, Will.

Q: Does the book start before, during or after the change?
A: After

The opening sequence

Q: What technique is used to pique the curiosity?
A: This is another example that uses a mix of several. There is an air of menace in the horrific nature of the attack, though it is not graphically described, and raises a question about what will happen to Nadifa as an asylum seeker whose claim has been refused and what has happened to her daughter who Nadifa managed to protect during the attack? In addition, there is an element of surprise in learning that Nadifa is in custody – why?

Q: Where is the opening sequence set?
A: In Cote d'Ivoire and in the detention centre in Manchester.

Q: Who is the main character in the opening sequence and how will you convey the necessary information e.g. age?
A: Nadifa. She is young – she has one young daughter and is pregnant. She is also brave – faced with the soldiers who attack her, she is determined to keep her daughter safe.

Q: What is happening and where? How will you convey this?
A: Nadifa's life is changed forever first by the attack on her, then by subsequent events, not fully explained, after she and her family escape to the UK. The first section conveys the heat and smell of death as Nadifa faces the soldiers, the second the cold bleakness of the detention centre at night as Nadifa cares for her newborn son and realises that she can't love him.

How is the opening scene brought to a close?

Q: What is the decision / commitment made?
A: Nadifa decides, even though she has lost her husband and daughter, even though her situation seems hopeless, and even

though she can't love him, she will do everything she can to protect her new baby

Q: Which character makes this decision / commitment?
A: Nadifa.

The Last Room has a double opening scene – one set in Cote d'Ivoire in Africa, followed by a time jump to a few months later in Manchester, but both scenes form part of the same sequence and act as an opening to the novel.

You might come across guidelines that advise against using a double opening scene such as this. You might even be told that a double opening like this 'breaks the rules'. Certainly, a sudden switch from one place to another, or one character to another can lose a reader this early in a book, but don't discount the double opening. *The Last Room* pulls together the two parts in a way that heightens the readers' desire to read on, rather than losing their attention.

Toolkit for the opening sequence

Your turn now. Answer the questions below for your own novel.

The start point

What is the change?	
What are the potential consequences?	
Who will be affected by these?	

Having decided the nature of the change, the potential consequences and who will be affected, think through the options of exactly where to start.

Will your novel start before, during or after the change?	

Now fill in the gaps below in relation to the first few paragraphs:

The opening sequence

What technique(s) will you use to pique the curiosity?	
Where is the opening sequence set?	
Who is the main character in the opening sequence and how will you convey the necessary information e.g. age?	
What is happening and where? How will you convey this?	

How is the opening scene brought to a close?

What is the decision / commitment made?	
Which character makes this decision / commitment?	

The information above gives you all the components you need to write a compelling opening sequence. Once you have drafted it, check that you have NOT:

- introduced too many characters
- switched viewpoint
- included the characters' back stories
- misled the reader
- gone into flashback.

Advanced techniques

Fiction writers put language together to create compelling stories. One of the major hooks into a story is the human desire we all have to know what happens next.

In the following sections, some of the techniques outlined earlier in the chapter will be looked at with a close focus on the way the writer has used language.

Raise a question in the readers' minds.

There are many ways of doing this. Here are some specific techniques.

Technique 1

Begin with a pronoun (he, she, it, they etc). Pronouns usually indicate shared information between the reader and the writer. In the first sentence of a novel, there is no shared information so this is a) unexpected and b) makes the reader ask a question. It should be intriguing enough to make them read on to find the answer, but don't keep them in suspense too long – the technique can irritate if it's overdone.

It had been a game at first.

This is the opening sentence from *Night Angels*. It raises the questions, What was a game? What is happening? It also raises a supplementary question: So isn't it a game? This implies it is serious. This technique can also be used to create a sense of menace (see later for further detail). The first paragraph from *Night Angels* is:

> *It had been a game at first. The dark BMW had pulled out of the car park behind her and followed her along the main road back into the centre of Manchester. 'Bloated plutocrat,' she'd muttered, using the epithet she'd heard Luke use when he saw someone in possession of some consumer item he, in truth, coveted. The BMW had followed her back on to the motorway, and the driver hadn't, to her surprise, used the capacity of his car to vanish once the three lanes opened up in front of him. Or at least she kept seeing its dark sleekness, sometimes in front, sometimes behind, but never far away. She began to look in the mirror more closely, trying to see the driver to see if it was the same car each time. The windows were tinted – pretentious git. Another Lukeism. She got the impression of fair hair – blond? White? She couldn't tell.*

Technique 2

Start in the middle of something. Readers have a subconscious expectation that a narrative will begin at the beginning, go on to the end, then stop, though very few actually do this. If you begin in the middle, maybe of an on-going event, maybe of another text altogether, a letter or a diary for example, the reader will ask the question: What is this? What's happening?

It's important to arouse curiosity, but not to confuse. If you confuse readers, they are unlikely to continue with the book.

Later in the week we were given orders to clear the area.

This is the opening sentence from *The Forest of Souls*. The opening paragraph is visually different from the main text which shows the reader they are not yet in the main body of the book. The opening sentence uses a pronoun in a way that appears to assume the readers know what the writer is talking about: *we*. It also uses the definite article, 'the' which also suggests the readers already know what is being talked about.

This raises questions: Who is included in this 'we'? What area? How is it to be cleared? Where are we?

The rest of the paragraph answers some of these questions, but sets up more as the text draws back, and the reader realizes he or she is effectively reading over someone's shoulder, looking at a wartime diary written by a Nazi occupier.

Later in the week, we were given orders to clear the area. That night, they firebombed the houses and left the streets burning. I watched as the work progressed. Towards midnight, a woman with a young child in her arms ran towards the gates. She was stopped by a policeman who seized the child, who was perhaps a year old, struck it against the wall then threw it into the flames. He shot the mother dead.

I very much wish to be home.

Open with something unexpected

> *Frank Stout was a serial killer. He didn't mean to be – he'd always planned to be an accountant. But instead, he became a serial killer who raised maggots.*
> *This is how it happened.*

This is the opening from *No Flies on Frank*. Readers bring certain expectations to books. Serial killer narratives rarely introduce the killer at the opening. This should be the ending, the denouement: It was Frank all the time!

A further way in which this opening is unexpected is by the use of an opening more often found in oral narratives: *This is how it happened*. It's saying overtly: I'm going to tell you a story. Kurt Vonnegut uses this technique in his book *Slaughterhouse 5*:

> *Listen! Billy Pilgrim has come unstuck in time.*

In the case of *No Flies on Frank*, both the opening devices alert the reader to the fact that the story itself will not be entirely serious.

Create a sense of menace

The extract from *Night Angels*, above, not only makes the reader ask questions, it creates a sense of menace in the way the words are chosen. Remember that you share a cultural context with your readers. What you know, they know. Here, the writer has used shared knowledge about a brand of car and combined it with the technique of personification to add menace to the scene. Gemma is being stalked, not by a person, but by a black

BMW with tinted windows. Ask anyone what they might associate with such a vehicle, and they might respond as Gemma does: a rich person, a pretentious person, but they also know BMWs are often marketed as a man's car. The slogan 'ultimate driving machine' that was current when this book was published was designed to appeal to a male market. Though the car is personified by making it perform human actions, it also depersonalises whoever is driving the car. Gemma is being stalked by a machine, and machines have no mercy and no compassion.

Gemma has been put in a vulnerable situation, one that readers will identify with. She's driving alone at night. She knows this. She's frightened. Something is wrong. BMWs are fast, powerful cars, but this one is being driven slowly. All of these devices signal to the reader that something is about to go terribly wrong.

Something out of the ordinary

This is the first paragraph from *Syrup Trap City*:

Maximilian Corder would have walked past the restaurant without a thought had a waft of fresh coffee not tickled his nostrils. "Hull's premier cup of coffee," a sign proclaimed. He didn't want a hot drink, but he slowed. The long strides that had brought him this far had boosted his circulation, suffused him with the certainty that it was good to be alive. If he carried on at this speed he would be early and have to wait. He didn't do waiting. It made sense to stop for a drink. And anyway, he enjoyed watching people squirm.

Here is a man on a mission, striding through a city's streets – the city of Hull, we learn from the mention of the sign – and he decides he has time to stop for a drink. So far, so ordinary. And note that a certain impression is given of Max Corder – *long strides, suffused with certainty*. He's tall, he's confident, and he's not a patient type – *he didn't do waiting*.

But it's his secondary reason for stopping for a drink – *he enjoyed watching people squirm* – that makes this out of the ordinary, more than just a man stopping at a coffee bar.

Surprise the reader

There is an interesting aspect of language known as 'collocation'. Certain words are very often associated with other words. This can run from clichés like 'as warm as toast' or 'a carpet of flowers' to more everyday combinations. The word 'fast' goes with or collocates with food, train and car for example. It doesn't go so comfortably with 'meal'. We have fast food and a quick meal. The idea of collocation is a very useful one for writers. You can use unexpected collocations of words, of events, and of ideas.

In the opening to *No Flies on Frank* above, the combination of the phrase 'serial killer' and 'by accident' is an unusual collocation. It is incongruous and as well as surprising the readers, it alerts them to the fact that the story will not be entirely serious.

Another example of unexpected collocation is in the opening of *The Forest of Souls*, above. The combination of horrendous events: *firebombed, seized the child, flames, shot, dead* contrasts with the emotionless way the diarist responds: he is simply a camera. 'I watched.' The extract ends with the contrasting image of 'home'. In this case, the unexpected collocations don't create humour, they create menace and horror.

We now have a reader who is committed to the book. Our job as authors is to ensure that the story doesn't disappoint.

CHAPTER THREE

The scene that builds tension

This chapter will look at
- the scene of rising tension and how it is constructed
- what to include and what to leave out
- how to build towards a cliff hanger chapter ending
- the use of cinematic techniques in writing.

The scene that builds tension in overview

The scene that builds tension happens in real time. A character in the scene is shown to have a goal; they pursue it, but meet with opposition that forces them into a change of plan. They amend their plan and this is the place to show your main character's traits, good and bad. The scene builds to a punch line that signifies some kind of disaster in terms of the original goal.

You can vary the level of tension built within the scene. The tighter the viewpoint, the more tension you build. Rising-tension scenes are strictly show-don't-tell. When you are building tension in a scene, keep to real time, don't inadvertently summarize the action; the reader must live it with the characters. That means no flashback.

Write big in rising-tension scenes.

Constructing the rising-tension scene

Establishing the landscape

This is a scene in which you grab the reader at the start and hustle them along into the action, not allowing them to draw breath until the scene is over. Thus you must not leave your reader wondering where or when this action is happening. Establish the time, the place, and the circumstances and make clear who is the viewpoint character right at the start of a scene.

Don't say where the scene is played out, SHOW it. Likewise with the time of day or night. Don't say that it's dark, have your character struggle to see in the fading light. Don't tell the reader where your character is, show your character stumbling on the rough ground or feeling the salt tang of the sea breeze.

Establishing the goal

Because this is commercial fiction and not real life, someone always has a goal in a rising-tension scene. In order to write a good compelling scene, you need to be clear about the goal; whose it is, what it is and why it is so urgent. It is usually the viewpoint character's goal, but not always.

Most goals fall into one of three categories: the goal to have something; the goal to get away from or get free of something; and the goal to get revenge for something.

Whatever the goal is, there has to be a level of urgency to achieve it. If there's no urgency, you won't be able to build tension around it. So work out why it is important for this character to pursue this goal now.

Having worked out all this, you must now develop your character's initial plan to achieve the goal.

What gets in the way of the goal?

Because this is commercial fiction and we are writing a rising-tension scene, something will get in the way of the character's plan.

This is the place to show off your character's strengths. Your character needs to be strong to be able to overcome the opposition. Decide what specific capability or strength they will demonstrate in order to do so.

Now work out what it is that obstructs your character's plan. And how does your character get to know about it? A useful trick is to identify through which sense this information arrives. Does your character see it, hear it, feel it, smell it, taste it …? By identifying the sense, you give yourself a big reminder to show the action, to allow the reader to live it with the character.

A rising-tension scene is a good place to add in your plot twists – something unanticipated by the reader and usually by the character. Something to add an extra pinch of spice to the story.

You are already showing off your character's strengths in this scene, but you can also show extra character traits here too if they are relevant to the action of the scene.

Having had his or her plan obstructed, the character must adjust the plan. It is your job to work out what adjustment they make.

The cliff hanger

The scene of rising tension builds to a climax. It ends on a cliff hanger. Generally speaking this is because something happens that is disastrous to the planned goal. Something new comes along that is unanticipated by your character. Whatever this new information is, it must be logical. If it isn't logical it will just look like a contrived device to create a moment of high tension and is more likely to irritate the reader than to have them turning the page.

A useful way to keep focus is to write the final dramatic moment of your scene and then use the other elements to write towards it.

Beware a problem that can occur before you get the hang of this. You might write a dramatic line that is too far ahead in the story so when you try to write the scene, it is very hard to reach it. Often this is because you have failed to milk the potential drama and what you really need are several scenes both building and releasing tension before you arrive at the dramatic moment you had originally identified. There is more later in the book on how to milk those dramatic moments. Dramatic moments and scenes of rising-tension often take many more words to write than you first anticipate.

Worked example from a scene near the end of *Like False Money*

Q: Who is the viewpoint character?
A: Annie.

Q: Where is the scene played out?
A: On the cliffs above the North Sea in East Yorkshire – feel the wetness of the rain and the noise of the storm.

Q: What time of day / night?

A: Evening, turning to night – show darkness creeping in.

Q: What are the circumstances?

A: She has to go with Mally because she has no way to stop her.

Goal

Q: Whose goal (usually the viewpoint character)?

A: Annie's.

Q: What is it (usually possession of, relief from or revenge for)?

A: To get the information from Mally and then get the police.

Q: What is the urgency?

A: The missing girl is on borrowed time.

Q: What is the immediate plan?

A: To go with Mally until she can get at the information Mally is holding back.

Conflict

Q: What is the opposition (why does the main character have to be strong)?

A: Mally's stubbornness and refusal to tell Annie what she knows.

Q: What is the main character's specific capability / strength?

A: Her ability to empathize with a hostile teenager.

Q: What obstructs the plan and through which sense does this information arrive?

A: Mally going to pieces when she realizes the significance of where she's leading Annie. Annie hears it in Mally's voice.

Q: Optional: are there any unanticipated twists?
A: Realization she hasn't been led to the information needed to find the missing girl, but to the girl herself.

Q: Optional: are any extra character traits shown?
A: Annie's bravery in putting herself on the line because help won't come soon enough.

Q: How is the plan adjusted?
A: The plan is now to get the girl away before the killer comes back.

Disaster

Q: What is the disaster (usually new information – unanticipated but logical)?
A: Realization that someone else is nearby and she hasn't got the girl to safety.

Q: What is the punch line?
A: Through the rush and roar of the storm and the waves lashing the shore, Annie heard a tiny sound, like the snapping of a twig in the darkness beyond the wall.

Worked example from a scene in the middle of *The Last Room*

Q: Who is the viewpoint character?
A: Dariusz.

Q: Where is the scene played out?
A: In Dariusz's flat.

Q: What time of day / night?
A: Night. It's dark.

Q: What are the circumstances?
A: Dariusz is grieving for the death of his lover, Ania. The police claim she committed suicide, but Dariusz knows she was murdered and there has been a cover-up. He thinks she found dangerous information, and may have hidden some links to it on his computer.

Goal

Q: Whose goal (usually the viewpoint character)?
A: Dariusz's.

Q: What is it (usually possession of, relief from or revenge for)?
A: To find the information Ania died for.

Q: What is the urgency?
A: His belief that someone else is on the track of this and will destroy it.

Q: What is the immediate plan?
A: To search his computer.

Conflict

Q: What is the opposition (why does the main character have to be strong)?
A: He doesn't know what he is looking for, where it may be or how to identify it.

Q: What is the main character's specific capability / strength?
A: His belief in Ania.

Q: What obstructs the plan and through which sense does this information arrive?

A: The sheer difficulty of checking every single file and programme, and the fact that time is running out.

Q: How is the plan adjusted?

A: He realises a way to simplify his search.

Disaster

Q: What is the disaster (usually new information – unanticipated but logical)?

A: Someone has hidden a video, a deeply incriminating one, deep in his system.

Q: What is the punch line?

A: As he is trying to come to terms with what he has found, the police arrive and raid his flat.

Toolkit for the scene that builds tension

Your turn now. Pick a scene of rising tension from your work and figure out the components by answering the questions below.

Who is the viewpoint character?	
Where is the scene played out?	
What time of day / night?	
What are the circumstances?	

Goal

Whose goal (usually the viewpoint character)?	
What is it (usually possession of, relief from or revenge for)?	
What is the urgency?	
What is the immediate plan?	

Conflict

What is the opposition (why does the main character have to be strong)?	
What is the main character's specific capability / strength?	
What obstructs the plan and through which sense does this information arrive?	
Optional: are there any unanticipated twists?	
Optional: are any extra character traits shown?	
How is the plan adjusted?	

Disaster

What is the disaster (usually new information – unanticipated but logical)?	
What is the punch line?	

Now you have the components for the scene and are ready to write it, but remember that you need to establish time, place, circumstance, and viewpoint at the start. Show these things, don't tell them. Showing makes the action more immediate. Make it clear that a character has a goal. Don't write small. This is where the reader is right on the shoulder of the viewpoint character experiencing the action in real time. Don't slip into flashback. Beware of accidentally summarizing. Your character and your reader need to race or inch step by step through the action together.

Was your scene already written but you weren't satisfied with it? Picking out the individual components will show you if there is anything in there that shouldn't be. Have you used flashback? Have you drifted from the point of this particular scene? Is your character's goal clear enough?

Advanced techniques

Cinematic techniques

In the previous chapter, we looked at ways of using the cultural knowledge that reader and writer share. 21st century readers and writers are familiar with the way the camera is used in film and TV narrative to create a range of effects. Screenwriters don't need to describe the action in the way a prose fiction writer does, the camera will do the job for them.

Writing for a camera-literate audience opens up a range of techniques for the writer. Readers bring their expectations of camera techniques to books and are responsive to them. In moments of high tension, using camera techniques can be very effective.

Take particular note the next time you watch an extract from a suspense film or drama series. Look at the way the camera pulls back to give you the whole scene (equivalent to the omniscient narrator: the camera and the audience can see more than the protagonist). Look at the way the camera moves in close so that the viewer can see only what the main character sees. Tension comes from the awareness that out of sight, something dangerous may be lurking.

Two screen texts that make very good use of these techniques are the film *Alien*, and the TV drama series *Buffy the Vampire Slayer*.

Using words as a camera

There are a lot of ways a writer can put language together to create tension. You can build up a sentence, using it almost like a camera pan to draw the reader through the scene:

The following extracts are from *Strangers*. Damien becomes aware that his journey to find his lover, Amy, has brought him unexpectedly into danger. The reader walks with him, listening to the same sounds, sharing the same growing sense of peril.

As he moved along the walkway, he passed the front doors that were firmly shut, windows with the curtains pulled across and no glimmer of light showing, as though the inhabitants had decided to hide themselves away from the night.

As Damien draws closer to his destination, the door of Amy's flat, the 'camera' moves into close-up. Now, the reader can only focus on the door of Amy's flat. We don't see what is happening behind us, or what is happening beyond the door.

The door of her flat was a dark shadow, closed like all the others. He reached out and pushed it gently.

It swung open and the heavy beat poured out into the night.

Compare this way of writing with the way a writer from the pre-film period creates tension. The following extract is from *Bleak House*.

Sir Leicester is fidgety down at Chesney Wold, with no better company than the goat; he complains to Mrs Rouncewell that the rain makes such monotonous pattering on the terrace that he can't read the paper even by the fireside in his own snug dressing-room

"Sir Leicester would have done better to try the other side of the house, my dear," says Mrs Rouncewell to Rosa. "His dressing-room is on my Lady's side. And in all these years I never heard the step upon the Ghost's Walk more distinct than it is tonight!"

Here, Dickens uses the technique of foreshadowing (the reader has already been alerted to the significance of the sound of footsteps on the Ghost's Walk). He also creates a sense of immediacy by using the present tense. There is no 'camera' here though. The writing, through the dialogue, is descriptive, and may reflect the fact that in Dickens' time, visual stories were told via the medium of the theatre.

Tense scenes cannot be monotonous. Vary the length of your sentences. If you use a long, panning sentence consider ending the section on a short one.

Look at the following example from *Bleak Water*. Eliza's friend Maggie has died. Eliza has been clearing Maggie's flat. She's tired, she falls asleep. And then something wakes her.

First, the text uses a panning technique:

But she could feel the chill drifting down the corridor from the small kitchen. She felt her way along the corridor and into the off-shot. The cold was intense. Her eyes were becoming accustomed to the darkness now, and she could see a lighter rectangle that was the open door. It was a second before her mind took it in.

Then the camera comes back for a close up on the door:

The open door. The back door was open.

Language techniques

As well as varying sentence length, you can experiment with sentence structure to create different effects. You can create emphasis by using incomplete sentences: *The open door.*

Sentences in English have a fairly fixed order. The subject usually comes first, followed by the verb, then the object if there is one (The dog bit the postman) and finally the part of the sentence called the adverbial which gives information about where, when or how. (The dog bit the postman in the leg, hard, suddenly.) Changing the order of a sentence can create some interesting effects. You need to be careful doing this. If you play around with the order of a sentence like 'He was strong,' you could write something like 'Strong he was.' Beware! This is the language of bad poetry, and the effect is usually funny, whether the writer intends it or not.

However, the adverbial can be moved. Because this is the more unexpected structure, it can create emphasis, and it can also be used to develop suspense. Look at the following sentences:

The door closed suddenly.
He saw the street was empty as he looked around him.

The adverbial part of the sentence can easily move to the front, and keep the reader in some suspense:

Suddenly (question: suddenly what?) the door slammed.
As he looked around him (question: what does he see?) he saw the street was empty.

Making the everyday strange

Bringing menace and danger into the day to day world allows the reader to put themselves into the scene. *This could happen to me!* Some locations are associated in people's minds with a certain amount of danger. For example, people are often alert at railway stations and airports. These are transitory places: no one belongs there, we are all passing through and everyone is, at some level, tense. *Will I miss my flight? Can I hear the announcements?*

Putting someone into one of these places at a time when they are deserted can create a real sense of danger. A deserted airport is an anomaly: something is wrong. A deserted railway station at night is a setting fraught with potential danger. You can allow readers to draw on their own imaginations here – they will all have their own deserted railway station in their minds. In the following example from *Only Darkness,* we have already followed Debbie through the deserted night time streets to the station.

She began to run towards the platform in case her train was in. She hurried down the covered ramp, and then, seeing there was no train on the platform, slowed down. Had she missed it, was it late?

The platform was empty, and she began to realise that there was something wrong with the light. It was yellow and flickering, not bright enough. The shadows in the corners were larger and darker, and the waiting room was black. She tried the door. Locked …

The wind caught the platform sign and sent it rattling on its chain against the pipework. The rain splashed on the rail and then stopped. The light flickered again, the strange, yellow light, and then there was silence.

Using archetypes

Taking advantage of shared cultural awareness can be effective. An archetype is a universal and recurring image, pattern, or motif representing a typical human experience. If your writing taps into the archetypes of the culture, you can use your readers' awareness of these to create any effects you wish.

In myth and folklore, evil is associated with darkness, depth (cellars, pits, railway tunnels), sometimes with high places (towers), extremes of temperature and solitariness. The following description comes from the epic poem *Beowulf* and describes Grendel's mere, the lair of the monsters.

> *They inhabit a secret land of wolf-infested slopes, windy headlands and dangerous pathways over the fenland, where mountain streams flow down under the darkness of the headland. The mere stands not far from here measured in miles. Frost covered trees hang over it, and every night there is a terrible thing to see, fire on the water. Not even the wisest of men know the bottom.*

Evil is close by. When you are writing a rising-tension scene, it can be useful to think of your characters inhabiting two worlds: the world of day to day reality, and the world of evil and darkness. As you move from one world to another, you can create tension by signalling to your readers you are about the make the move, as film directors often do with the use of music and sound.

Striking the right balance between intrigue and irritation

Your aim, especially when building tension and is to give your readers enough information to intrigue them, without giving the impression you're hiding anything. If it seems that something is hidden that the readers should know about, they will become irritated and that might be the last you see of them.

How do you strike that balance?

The trick is to be tight behind the character's eyes in a particular situation and work with what that character is seeing, hearing, feeling and thinking about. And if you are tight behind the character's eyes, then as long as the character wouldn't explicitly be thinking about or reflecting upon a particular something, then you can get away without letting the reader know about that something.

To use an extreme example: your viewpoint character is a man standing at the top of a cliff. Someone else arrives. Your character greets the new person in a manner that shows they know each other e.g. 'Hello, I wondered where you'd got to.' Then the new arrival tries to push your character off the cliff. Your character clearly knows who this would-be assassin is, but in that situation the only thing in his mind for those first fractions of seconds will be the fight not to fall off the edge, the struggle to stay in balance, the frantic grabbing for a handhold. The reader might be desperate to know who it is, especially if this scene happens well into the novel, but it's fine not to say, as long as you stay very closely with your character as they struggle not to fall.

Of course, the very second your character reaches safety or has the tiniest opportunity to draw breath, feel anger, or reflect in any way, then he will think about who it was who tried to kill him. At this point you need to let the reader know.

But what if you don't want the reader to know yet?

Easy, cut to a new scene either before your character reaches the point where that something would pop into their head and have to be revealed to the reader. Or you can really up the tension by cutting the scene at the exact point the information is about to be revealed.

Rising-tension scenes are crucial, but it's equally important to be able to release that tension, to give the reader a breather, without losing anything from the gripping narrative.

CHAPTER FOUR

The scene that releases tension

This chapter will look at
- the scene that releases tension and how it is constructed
- the ebb and flow of building and releasing tension through the novel and how to link scenes
- how to control pace and why it is sometimes better to tell than to show
- advanced techniques for releasing tension.

The scene that releases tension in overview

This is the structure to release tension following the drama of the rising-tension scenes. These are the scenes where you can have flashback, time jumps and where you can compress long stretches of time. These scenes are the places for detailed description to add credibility.

However, the tension-releasing scene does not stand still. It shows a character's reaction to the dramatic events of a rising-tension scene; it presents a character with a dilemma in relation to the plot and it forces them into a decision about what to do next.

In tension-releasing scenes you distance the reader from the thick of the action, you allow them to sit back and reflect with the characters. One way to do this is to tell them what is going on, i.e. tell-don't-show: a complete reverse of the mantra you will have heard many times. Show-don't-tell brings a reader close to the action. Sometimes you want the reader to sit back and review the action. Hence tell-don't-show can be better when you are writing a tension-releasing scene. One area where tell-don't-show works especially well is in describing the main character's state of mind in this type of scene.

The ebb and flow of scenes through the novel

Tension-releasing scenes follow on from rising-tension scenes and vice versa, but they might not follow directly. The book might have several strands and sub-plots, each with its own series of rising-tension and tension-releasing scenes. In order not to cut the reader adrift, you must show which scenes link together.

If you have just made a big time jump, you don't want to leave the reader floundering over when and why. The way to add a link to a tension-releasing scene is to make a specific reference back to the rising-tension scene to which it relates. This might be a reference to an object, a place, a character's state of mind or something to remind the reader of the dramatic conclusion.

It is different for the rising-tension scene because although you still want the reader to know which scenes link together, the link is already there. At the end of the tension-releasing scene, your character will make a decision. This becomes the goal for the next rising-tension scene in the sequence.

Constructing the tension-releasing scene

Establishing the context

In establishing the context, you need to know the who, the when, and the where. Who is the main character in this scene? When does the scene take place? Note that the scene can stretch across a long time. When you describe where this scene takes place, remember that detail adds credibility. This does not mean description for the sake of it, but a description of unusual details can bring a scene to life.

It is important in establishing the context to make sure you link this scene back to the rising-tension scene to which it is relevant. Do this by mentioning an item, a mood, a particular person or anything that will jog the readers' memories and remind them where this scenes fits in.

Describing the reaction

Having established the context you now need to show the character's reaction to the dramatic events of the relevant rising-tension scene.

What is the character's state of mind? Remember to TELL this, don't show it. This will help to keep the right pace and mood in this tension-releasing scene.

This is also the place to describe the views and reactions of other characters. Make sure you do this from the viewpoint character's point of view. Experiment with mixtures of show and tell. These will vary from scene to scene. You will learn to judge the right mix to give a particular pace and mood.

What is the dilemma?

Because this is commercial fiction your character will be faced with a dilemma of some sort as a result of the preceding dramatic events. Identify the courses of action open to your character.

Making a decision

Your character has choices and has to decide between them. How and why will they make this decision? The decision they make will become the goal for the next rising-tension scene in the sequence.

Do not have your characters make decisions without any reason. It should always be clear why they make a particular decision. Sometimes for the purposes of the plot they will need to make what appear to be bad or foolish decisions. Always make sure that there is a reason for your character to have been pushed in a particular way.

Worked example From *The Jawbone Gang*

Q: **Who** is the main character in this tension-releasing scene?
A: Annie.

Q: **When** does this take place?
A: In the early hours.

Q: **Where** does this take place? Detail adds credibility
A: In the farmhouse kitchen (describe the sleepy reactions from the dogs, the photos on the mantelpiece).

Q: **What is the link** back to the scene (a mood, an item…)?
A: The location and the presence of the Morgans. She is in the Morgans' kitchen. The preceding rising-tension scene left her facing the Morgans in the barn.

Reaction

Q: What is the main character's state of mind (**tell**, don't show)?
A: In shock but also numb.

Q: What is the main character's reaction to the events of the preceding scene?
A: Still feels the terror of what happened in the barn and is trying to work out if what she's seeing now is the truth or not.

Q: What are the views / reactions of others?
A: Shocked at Annie being there but also relieved at having someone to tell.

Dilemma

Q: What courses of action are there?
A: Annie must decide which way to use this to wrap up the case for her clients back in Hull – to do what Ron wants or to do what Cheryl wants or to take some other course.

Decision

Q: What **decision** is made?
A: To leave the clients in limbo until she knows more about their real agenda.

Q: Why is the main character pushed this way?
A: Her own code of ethics: she won't report anyone when she has no evidence of a crime but she won't give them free rein to cause mayhem either.

Worked example from *Life Ruins*

Q: **Who** is the main character in this tension-releasing scene?
A: Becca.

Q: **When** does this take place?
A: In Bridlington, the morning after a serious attack on a teenage girl.

Q: **Where** does this take place? Detail adds credibility
A: Outside the police station in Bridlington after Becca has been interviewed. Describes Becca's first brief meeting with Jared in the waiting room, Becca's hostile attitude towards the police, her determination to help in case the injured girl is her friend Paige.

Q: **What is the link** back to the scene (a mood, an item…)?
A: The presence of Jared who is also there to talk to the police, having been a witness to the attack the night before. Becca and Jared are not yet aware that they are connected via the attack.

Reaction

Q: What is the main character's state of mind (**tell**, don't show)?
A: Angry, frightened of the police given her previous encounters with them, frightened for Paige.

Q: What is the main character's reaction to the events of the preceding scene?
A: Frightened for Paige who went off in a strange car the night before, before the attack was reported. Angry that the police don't seem to be doing enough and won't give her the information she needs.

Q: What are the views / reactions of others?
A: The police simply want the information she has, Jared is curious about her.

Dilemma

Q: What courses of action are there?
A: Becca has to decide whether to return to work where things are not going well, or whether to drive Jared, who is recovering from a serious injury, back to the caravan site on the coast where the attack took place (though Becca is not aware of the connection at this time).

Decision

Q: What **decision** is made?
A: Becca decides to drive Jared to the coast.

Q: Why is the main character pushed this way?
A: She is tired of people telling her what to do and not taking her seriously, she is also concerned for Jared.

Toolkit for the tension-releasing scene

Your turn now. Answer the questions below using a tension-releasing scene from your novel.

Who is the main character in this tension-releasing scene?	
When does this take place?	
Where does this take place (detail here will add credibility)?	
What is the link back to the rising-tension scene (a mood, an item…)?	

Reaction

What is the main character's state of mind (**tell**, don't show)?	
What is the main character's reaction to the events of the preceding scene?	
What are the views / reactions of others?	

Dilemma

What courses of action are there?	

Decision

What **decision** is made (becomes the goal for the next rising-tension scene)?	
Why is the main character pushed this way?	

Use the elements above either to write the scene or, if you already have it drafted, to see if you can sharpen it up.

Advanced techniques

Pulling back the camera

Look at the extracts in the previous chapter where tension is developed. They use a range of techniques: camera techniques of panning and close-up, language techniques including long and short sentences, and bringing the adverbial to the front. They also draw on the archetype of the otherworld as a place of evil.

In the follow-up scenes, the tension is reduced. In the next chapter of *Strangers*, the narrative has moved to a different scene. One of the main characters, Roisin is at home looking after a friend's baby.

Roisin had settled Adam to sleep. She tried to get on with what she had been doing, but kept stopping to check on him. It must be like this bringing a new baby home for the first time, the sudden awareness that she was the sole carer for this child, overwhelmed by his vulnerability and fragility. She realized that all the jokes about new parents hanging over their babies' cribs to see if the child was still breathing were simply true.

She could hear the faint snuffle of his breath. His face was serene and his tiny fists were close to his face. She resisted the temptation to pick him up again. It wouldn't be fair to disturb him just to satisfy a need in her that was deep and growing.

The pace of the section is slow. The writing is from Roisin's point of view, but her thoughts and emotions are all on the surface. When a writer is creating tension, the writing is often implicit – not everything is explained, the camera has pulled in for a tight close-up, and the reader is not sure what is going on around this main scene. In scenes that release tension, the camera has pulled back and writing is more explicit. It doesn't make the reader ask too many questions, or try to work out what is happening beyond the scene.

The style reduces the tension. The sentences are of similar length, and the order of the sentences is the expected one. The scene also draws on archetypes of mother and child: a sleeping child and a nurturing woman create a sense of peace.

Allowing the reader and the characters to look forward

The section above from *Strangers* also allows the book to look forward. It explores Roisin's desire for a child, something that is only touched on in the main narrative, but adds an extra dimension to the understanding of the character and her subsequent actions.

In *Bleak Water*, the follow up to the high tension scene is one that helps to move the narrative on. Eliza is interviewed by the police officer in charge of the investigation, a man who has also become a friend. In the previous scene, we have been looking through Eliza's eyes at a series of images that caused tension and fear. Here the camera has pulled back and we are watching a relatively static scene through the analytical eyes of Roy Farnham.

Again, the style reduces the tension. The sentences are fairly long and of similar length. There are no foregrounded adverbials and nothing in the style to surprise or puzzle the reader. The scene also takes the opportunity to sum up events in a fast-moving narrative before the pace quickens again.

'Are you sure about that, Eliza? Do you need to go over it again?' Farnham watched Eliza carefully as she shook her head. She'd had a shock on top of the shock of finding Stacy McDonald's body; she'd had two broken nights and she had been cold and panicked when she'd called him. But she looked calm now, seemed very certain about what she was saying.

We have now covered the ebb and flow of the story through the book, hopefully gripping the reader throughout. The next step is to give them a satisfying conclusion.

CHAPTER FIVE

Bringing the story to a satisfying end

This chapter will look at
- the climax and resolution to the story
- how and when to tie loose ends
- how to leave the reader feeling they've had a good read
- techniques to make the ending feel just right.

The climax and resolution in overview

The sequence where the rising tension in the book reaches its climax and is then resolved often turns out to be the penultimate chapter. The closing chapter is then left for the resolution, the last tying of loose ends and a satisfying final sequence to leave the reader feeling that they've had a good read.

How to construct the climax and resolution

Never underestimate the importance of a good ending to a book. The reader might have been grabbed mercilessly by the opening and then riveted by the story as it unfolded, but if the ending is flat or disappointing you might put them off coming back for more.

This is commercial fiction, not real life. Clear the decks for a dramatic conclusion. That means you should tie the loose ends from any subplots before you reach the final sequence. Concentrate only on the major plot and the peripheral angles that impact upon it.

Note that tying loose ends does not mean tying every single one and explaining everything. Readers want realism. Real life doesn't tie loose ends. However, beware leaving your readers frustrated by something that has just been left hanging.

The climax and resolution is a building of tension, a culmination of all the tension building within the novel, but now the stakes are significantly higher. The main character has to get through this one. The action reaches a climax. Then the story resolves itself and the characters receive their reward (or punishment) in line with poetic justice. This should leave the reader with the satisfying feeling of justice having been done, the right result having been achieved. All that is left then is to wind up the book with a final sequence showing that the characters have a future and those who deserve it have achieved fulfilment.

How to build to a climax

The way to build to a dramatic climax is to set up a situation where your character is faced with a very clear choice or choices. There must be a significant goal behind these choices, something that chimes with one of the character's main traits that will have been apparent throughout the novel. This character will be making a choice based upon principle.

Similarly to the rising-tension scene there will be an urgency behind the need to choose. You need to work out why your character has to make a quick decision. You also need to be very clear about your character's motivation so you can make it credible to the reader that the character has to choose. There will be good and bad choices in front of the character and something will push them one way or another. Very often the choice will appear to be a very bad one to other characters in the story, but the character making the choice will be doing it for principled reasons.

If there is insufficient urgency to make the decision, there will be insufficient drama to hold the scene. Apart from making this a principled decision and making it a decision that the character has to make very quickly, you should further increase the tension by making it a decision that cannot be undone once it has been made. This usually means that the character makes the decision quickly, then acts upon it and it may not be until this point that it becomes clear there is no going back.

How to create the resolution

Your character has now made a choice and has acted upon this decision. It is too late to go back. Now is the point to have the character realise the full implications of the decision made so quickly. Very often at this point of the story the character will appear to be in a hopeless position, perhaps unable to avoid death at the hands of the killer, or maybe irrevocably estranged from the love of their life.

This being commercial fiction, a hopeless situation can be reversed. But the days are gone when the character can get out of trouble 'in one mighty bound …' Something will happen that just tips the balance and allows the character, because of their strengths and skills, to find a way out at the last moment. Whatever the something is, it should be unanticipated by the main character, and ideally unanticipated by the reader too.

However it must be logical. It cannot be something coming out of a blue sky. Use something that has been seeded earlier and bring it out at the crucial moment.

When the situation is resolved and the crisis has passed, the characters should receive their reward or their punishment according to what they deserve. The usual reward for characters is to allow them to achieve their goal. However the true reward will satisfy an emotional need within the character and not just a material need. This is usually the point for them to realise that the goal they had been chasing was not what they truly wanted. So to reward them properly you will allow them to achieve their real goal.

In *Like False Money* Annie is presented with the opportunity to achieve the dream she's chased of a good job with security, but once it's there for the taking, she realizes that what she really wants is autonomy and the chance to build something for herself.

The loose ends

Most of the loose ends that should have been tied will have been tied before the climax and resolution begin. However there may yet be some that are integral to how your main character finally reached his or her goal. These need to be dealt with because if you leave them hanging it will feel to the reader like cheating. In the end your main character needs to make it through his or her own efforts, not by chance or luck. Tie these last loose ends before the novel finishes. Remember though that if you painstakingly tie every single one in a neat knot, you are in danger of making the story just too unrealistic. Real life always leaves loose ends. But you must judge which it is safe to leave untied. If there is a particular loose end that you do not wish to tie, but which you think the reader will notice, then don't just leave it, because the reader will assume you have forgotten. Have one of your characters notice and wonder about it. That way you can leave it untied but not forgotten.

The all-important last page

All that now remains is to round off the book. You want to leave the reader feeling satisfied that they have had a good read. You want to leave them feeling that the danger for the characters is over and that the characters have a future. There are many ways to do this. Very often in tying up the climax and resolution you will already have tidied away the danger that the characters were in.

What you need to do is to signal that the characters themselves know that they are safe and that all is well. There are several ways to do this. You might seed some small thing from very early in the book, some item or mannerism or some way of conversing between two characters that signals to them that all is well. Be subtle about this along the way and then you can use it right at the end to give a satisfying end to the book.

Worked example From *The Jawbone Gang*

The climax – setting up the situation where your character has clear choices

Q: What are the choices?
A: Annie can legitimately stand back and wait for the emergency services to arrive or she can go in and try to calm the situation.

Q: What principle is at stake?
A: She feels responsible for what might happen to Eliza or to the children who could be trapped. This has come about because of an act of revenge on her.

Q: Is the goal important enough?
A: It's her integrity at stake and could affect her whole future.

Forcing your character to choose

Q: Why is the character forced to choose?
A: The necessity to choose comes from within. She has been painted as a character who would not dither in such a situation, although there is no external force pressuring her to do anything other than stand back.

Q: What tips the scales towards the right choice?
A: The knowledge that she could have foreseen this if she hadn't missed the signs she was being followed.

Making the decision irrevocable

Q: What is the act that makes the decision irrevocable?
A: To go into the buildings to confront the woman who's waiting for her.

Q: Why is there no turning back?
A: The woman who intends to destroy herself and everyone around her will be pushed to act if Annie tries to turn back.

The resolution that rewards or punishes according to poetic justice

Q: What makes the character despair initially over their decision now it is made?
A: Annie realizes that it is her presence that will spark the disaster and she should have waited out of sight to buy time.

Q: How is the situation reversed (should be desired, unanticipated and logical)?
A: The sight of Eliza clutching a pen reminds her of the diaries and she realizes the significance of what she read. She can use this to gain the fraction of a second she needs.

Q: What is the reward (it must satisfy an emotional need)?
A: Annie has a good result from her last case. She shows the strength of her ethical code by berating the bystanders who are ready to mete out summary justice.

Tying up the loose ends

Q: Have the loose ends from other sub plots been tied before the final scene begins?
A: Yes.

Q: Are there any loose ends relating to the drama of the final scene that must be explained?
A: The final loose end is to explain what made Annie shout to Eliza at the key moment because of what she had finally worked out about the old Jawbone Gang diaries. Note that this had to be seeded earlier in order for it to work, but that it gives a neat way to provide a final twist to the main plot.

The final paragraphs

Q: How is it signalled that danger is over and the main characters have a future?

A: In this book there is no subtlety about this: the bad guys are under lock and key; the people who could have been caught in the crossfire are safe and the final scene is set at the railway station showing Annie heading towards a better future.

Q: What is the final punch line and how does it signal fulfilment?

A: The finale is a call to Annie from her new partner. This gives the ending an upbeat tone. Note that the book could have ended as Annie waved goodbye to the Thompson sisters but this would have ended on a slightly downbeat note, whereas the phone call leaves her explicitly looking towards the future.

Toolkit for the final scene

Your turn now to set up your own final sequence. Answer the questions below in relation to your own novel.

The climax – setting up the situation where your character has clear choices

What are the choices?	
What principle is at stake?	
Is the goal important enough?	

Forcing your character to choose

Why is the character forced to choose?	
What tips the scales towards the right choice?	

Making the decision irrevocable

What is the act that makes the decision irrevocable?	
Why is there no turning back?	

The resolution that rewards or punishes according to poetic justice

What makes the character despair initially over their decision now it is made?	
How is the situation reversed (this should be desired, unanticipated and logical)?	
What is the reward (it must satisfy an emotional need)?	

Tying up the loose ends

Have the loose ends from other sub plots been tied before the final scene begins?	
Are there any loose ends relating to the drama of the final scene that must be explained?	

The final paragraphs

How is it signalled that danger is over and the main characters have a future?	
What is the final punch line and how does it signal fulfilment?	

Advanced techniques

Seeding the end in the beginning

A useful technique is to seed some apparently minor incident or character trait right at the start and then use it to round off the story. For example, maybe the main character has a pet cat and the pet cat, attuned to the moods of its owner, goes off its food when it senses unhappiness or tension. Make this little more than a throwaway line, something that the main character possibly sees as a bit of an irritant rather than a cause for worry.

At the very end, the cat can be shown tucking into a heap of food, which will be enough to signal to the reader that all is now well.

The rule of three

If you are going to seed something for later use in a novel, it is a good idea to mention it three times. This is enough for it to lodge in the readers' minds, but not enough to signal too clumsily that it is being seeded for future use.

The cat example above might appear in the opening sequence, then a couple more times through the tale, perhaps in a tension-releasing scene where the character can mull on his or her misfortune whilst watching the cat turn up its nose at a plate of fresh food, and again in a rising-tension scene where the reader can be taken through the character's frantic rush through her flat to find something; the cat interrupting with insistent demands to be fed; the hurried grabbing of a tin from a packed cupboard, maybe slamming the door on an avalanche of tinned food, cutting her finger on a sharp edge as she opens the tin; blood on her new top … then the cat stalking off, food untouched.

Having seeded the cat's behaviour, it can be brought on stage right at the end, where all it needs to do is enthusiastically devour its food to show that everything is fine. You might even add a small twist and have it sneak in behind everyone's backs to eat the fish pâté sandwiches that the main characters have painstakingly made for a picnic to cement their future plans.

We have now completed the structural journey through the book, from the pitch, through the opening, the highs and lows of rising and releasing tension, and on to the conclusion. But we're not quite finished. There are a few more areas to cover, topics that are important throughout the narrative.

CHAPTER SIX

Using the toolkits

....

This chapter will look at
- when you should and shouldn't adhere to the rules of standard English
- the complexities of convincing dialogue
- giving your prose an extra pizazz
- some practical ideas for using the toolkits.

Having the toolkits and using them will give you the elements you need to create a work of commercial fiction. They do not substitute for work on plotting, characterization, research and so on, but will help you to structure and analyse your work.

In this final chapter, we cover some areas that apply to all parts of a commercial novel and that will help you to build convincing characters and realistic worlds in which your readers can lose themselves.

Getting it right: when to use standard English, and when to break the grammar 'rules'

Published manuscripts need the spelling and punctuation to be accurate – that's a given.

But what about 'correct' grammar in the sense of standard

English? If you are writing serious non-fiction, then standard English is what you should use, but novels are different. Writers usually adopt a voice in novels, because they are writing from the point of view of a character. This book can't teach you how to write in standard English – but there are plenty of books and websites that can. The question is, when do you need to use standard English, and when do you need a more informal voice? In narrative fiction, especially with point of view writing, the non-standard, less formal voice is often best. But be careful: you need to be certain that when you break the 'rules' you are doing it for a reason – you haven't simply made a mistake.

This applies to dialogue of course (see the following section) but it can also apply to the narrative sections and the exposition. If the writing here is too formal, it can sound stilted and awkward.

The following example from *The Last Room* is a mixture of standard English and non-standard forms as it moves between dialogue, narrative and the perceptions of the main character, Will Gillen:

> *But it wasn't the storm that had woken him. His fingers groped for the phone and he was already half out of bed, his response automatic. 'Yes?' He checked his watch, noting the time of the call – 5 a.m.*
>
> *'Dad?'*
>
> *'Ania! What's wrong?'*
>
> *'Don't panic. I wanted to call you before you saw the papers.'*
>
> *'The … give me a minute, Ania, I was asleep.'*
>
> *'I know. I'm sorry it's so early, but we'll be boarding soon and I wanted to talk to you before …'*

Boarding? He was getting out of bed as she spoke. 'Just a second.' He put the phone down and went to the basin. His face looked back at him in the mirror, unshaven with shadows under his eyes. His hair stood out in a wild tangle, showing the first strands of grey that were starting to weave through the black. He turned on the cold water, hard, and pushed his face under the tap, a trick he'd used often in the past to bring himself to quick alertness. He came back towelling his head. 'OK. Tell me what's going on.'

Here, though the narrative is from Will's point of view, it isn't written in his voice. The narrative uses unmarked standard English with some informal features – the use of 'but' to start a sentence, for example. This section is very close to the opening of the novel, and the narrative is carrying a lot of information – that Will is used to being woken early by urgent phone calls, that he checks the time automatically, that he has a trick to wake himself up quickly. These early impressions are confirmed when the reader finds out that Will used to be a senior police officer. There is one place where Will's voice appears in the narrative, with the question *Boarding?* This alerts the reader to the fact that Ania's trip comes as a surprise to Will, but note that the word 'surprise' is never used. The dialogue contains features of spoken language – incomplete sentences, false starts, interruptions. The moves between standard and non-standard, slightly more formal and less formal helps to differentiate the dialogue from the narrative. This is an example of writing from a character's point of view without necessarily writing in the 'voice' of the character.

You can move between standard and non-standard forms to create tension or a sense of urgency. Look at these two examples:

- *She thought there was someone behind her, and turned quickly, but there was no one there.*
- *Behind her! She spun round. Nothing.*

The first one uses complete standard sentences. This style of writing may be better for the build-up of tension. The second, which uses short, incomplete sentences is closer to the 'voice' of the character, and may be better for when the tension is high and the reader is moving quickly through the narrative.

Varying sentence length and structure can create variety in your writing and give it rhythm and pace. School English lessons might have taught you never to open a sentence with 'and' or 'but'. However, the subtle emphasis of that 'and' or 'but' may give you the exact effect you want to create.

The English language is a wonderfully versatile and flexible tool. Make the most of it!

Dialogue: creating your characters' voices

Writing convincing dialogue is one of the most important skills to develop. This section will give you examples, ideas and tips that can be used along with the rest of the techniques described in this book.

You can use dialogue to create and develop character, move the plot along and introduce important background material. If the dialogue doesn't work, the book doesn't work.

Real speech vs convincing dialogue

There is a temptation to assume that to write convincing dialogue you should strive to make it the same as real speech. Here's why you shouldn't.

Look at this example of spoken language. It has been written down exactly as it was spoken from a conversation among a group of men:

Key:

(.) marks a short pause.

… indicates people talking over each other.

Hey I'll tell you what though y'know I went to er (.) to B and Q (.) y'know (.) and I went for some er Carlite finish (.) and cos though they well they an't seen but you know the little cottage upstairs I've been doing …

… mm (.) yes …

… a bit of plastering and I thought I'd go and get some Carlite finish (.) like y'know put Unibond on then I'd to buy some fucking Unibond …

… Never

… said I've give em five gallons (laughter) still got it an all at home

A right price it is

I know it is

Anyway I I (.) I I goes down there for some pla(.) er twenty kilo bags (.) I thought twenty kilo bags no prices anywhere in B and Q (.) so I just gets two bags like I thought well there's nowhere in fucking here for me to weigh these like so I takes a couple goes to counter (.) plaster board I get so many plaster boards an all

Now compare this to dialogue from a novel, *Life Ruins*:

It's closing time at a drop-in centre for homeless young people on the east coast. Becca, 20, works in the coffee bar. One of the users, Paige, is troubled. She has stayed behind and seems to want to talk to Becca:

'Have you finished?' Paige asked.

'Not yet. I've still got to clear up.'

Paige pulled a face. 'What do you want to do this for?' Her gesture encompassed the shabby café, the litter on the floor, and the tables, sticky with spilled drinks.

It was another question Becca was asking herself. 'I need the money.' But a different answer was close to the surface.

'Yeah, but ... there's lots of ways to get money. You going to do that now?'

Becca hesitated. It looked like Paige wanted to talk. Hannah had advised her about this – 'They can trust you, Becca. You're near their age. No one will get upset with you if you leave your work to talk to one of the users who wants something.'

She wasn't sure if Neil would agree, but it made sense to her. There wasn't much clearing up to do anyway – she could finish off tomorrow morning if she came in a bit early. 'It can wait,' she said.

Paige was still watching her, chewing her lip as if she was unsure about something. Her long fair hair hung round her face and tonight she was wearing a denim jacket and a micro skirt over stylishly ripped leggings. Her feet were thrust into ballet slippers. It was Saturday night clubbing gear, not walking the streets dress.

'Any parties tonight?' Becca asked, to break the silence.

'Why? You want to come?'

'No. Not tonight.' And not to any party in this dump. 'Where are you going?'

Paige shrugged. 'Mate's. So, you got your car?'

'Not tonight. I'm walking.'

'I'll walk with you,' Paige said.

Becca was surprised, but didn't say anything as she collected her jacket and her bag. As they left, Alek came to lock up behind them. Paige walked ahead, ignoring him but as Becca went past him he said so quietly she barely heard him, 'Look after her. Make sure she is safe, all right?'

She looked back at him. 'What do you ...?' But the door was already closing.

Think about the examples above:

1. What features do the two examples have in common? In what ways are they different?
2. Who is the audience for each example?
3. What is the function of each example?

These are the points to note:

The spoken language example uses

- short forms e.g. 'I'll' rather than 'I will', 'I've' rather than 'I have'.
- incomplete sentences e.g. 'Never'
- false starts and repetitions. Speakers often make false starts and correct what they are saying as they go e.g. 'I I (.) I I goes down there for some pla(.) er twenty kilo bags'
- current slang 'like' 'you know'

- references to the immediate environment that can't be understood by people who are not present e.g. 'cos though they well they an't seen but you know'
- pauses (.) and fillers like er and erm.

Conversation in novels uses some of these features. Most writers use short forms and incomplete sentences when they are writing dialogue, occasionally they will use false starts. They may also use current slang forms (like starting sentences with 'so') to give a sense of the age and character of the participants. This gives a sense of realism. Novelists are less likely to use fillers, pauses and references that can't be understood by people outside the conversation.

This makes sense if you consider the audiences and the functions for the different types of dialogue.

For a real life conversation the audience is the people taking part. The audience for dialogue in a novel is the reader.

The functions of a real-life conversation will vary – it may be social chat, or it may have a purpose like getting children ready for school and helping to find something.

In a novel, the characters are presented as talking to each other, but in fact, the writer is communicating with the reader. The function of dialogue in a novel is to move the narrative along, to create and develop character, and to introduce important background material.

Different ways of representing speech

There are a lot of ways you can represent your characters' speech in a novel. There is Direct Speech. This is when you use the exact words, usually in speech marks:

'I wasn't here last week,' she insisted.

There is Indirect Speech (sometimes called reported speech), where you report what the character said, rather than the exact words:

She insisted she had not been there the previous week.

Another form of speech representation is Free Indirect Speech. This is somewhere between Direct Speech and Indirect Speech. The words spoken are reported, but in a way that makes it closer to the speaking voice:

Of course she hadn't been there last week.

The value to the writer of Free Indirect Speech is that it allows subtle commentary on the truth or otherwise of what the character is saying. A good example comes from Vladimir Nabokov's *Lolita*, a first-person narrative, where Humbert Humbert is trying to gain control of his step-daughter after her mother has been killed. He is being interviewed:

Yes I would devote all my life to the child's welfare.

The reader knows, having been in Humbert's mind, that this is not his intention at all. You don't need to know the terms for these methods of speech representation, but it's useful to know they exist and you can experiment with them in your writing.

The 'Ian ejaculated, "Corks!"' problem

Many of us will remember from school a real old turkey of a writing exercise where we were asked to list all the alternatives to 'said'. We were then supposed to use as many of these as possible and vary them to make our writing more lively.

It will not have occurred to most of us at the time that the writers we enjoyed the most used a very limited number of alternatives to 'said' and seemed to prefer 'said' above all.

It is possible to write compelling prose where there is no verb attributing the speech at all for long stretches. This only works as long as you don't leave your readers counting back to work out who said what in a long stretch of unattributed dialogue.

We've said throughout this book that we do not believe in definitive writing 'rules'. What works for one writer will not necessarily work for another. The 'only use said' rule has been quoted often enough to make it a cliché of writing schools, but it's worth bearing in mind.

Sue Knight, a couple of whose works we have used to demonstrate specific points, uses a greater variety of speech tags than is generally deemed the norm. E.g. *Miranda regretted*. In the isolated examples, they might look odd. In the context of the world she builds within her books, they work. Note also that Barbara Pym, a successful and much admired writer, gets away with 'chortled' which some would have labelled a total no-no. Which only goes to show that the rules really are there to be broken, but you will only break them effectively once you understand why they're there in the first place.

Representing accents

Should you use spelling to represent accent? Dickens did. Emily Bronte did. Irvine Welsh does. If writers of that calibre do it, then why not?

The problem is, it can be intrusive. Irvine Welsh maintains the accent that fits the narrative voice. He doesn't switch between a standard narrative and a regional accent for speech. This has the effect of pulling the reader straight into the world of Renton et al.

Many people these days find Dicken's representation of accent distracting. And how many of us skip over Joseph's long and almost impenetrable pronouncements in Wuthering Heights? A useful alternative to representing accent throughout speech is to hint at the pronunciation and let the readers 'hear' the voice in their heads.

As always with writing, there are no hard and fast rules. If you do want to represent accent via spelling, make sure it's realistic. Welsh's Trainspotting is good example of where this is effective.

How to make your dialogue believable

Unrealistic dialogue is one of the things that pulls a reader right out of the story. How can anyone get lost in a fictional world when all the characters' speech is stilted and feels as though they are reading from scripts?

Here are some practical ways to make your dialogue believable:
- Use short forms and incomplete sentences, to create a realistic effect. Compare: 'Oh, just a letter,' he said, with

'Oh, I have just received a letter.' But be careful the
dialogue doesn't get confusing.

- Write the dialogue on its own without any narrative.
Then add in the narrative detail. You often need far less
narrative than you expect.

- Remember who your characters are: Would they say
this? Would they use this particular vocabulary? Is this
right for the age/group/background of this character?

- Be careful with 'reporting' verbs (words like 'said,' or
'shouted' that are used with dialogue). You will rarely
need more than 'said', 'answered' and possibly one like
'shouted' to suggest volume.

- When you have written a stretch of dialogue, read it out
loud. Does it sound convincing?

From *Waiting for Gordo*:

*'Wake up, Miranda.' Miranda stared dazed at Jim smiling
down at her.*

*'Jim ... I was calling for you. There was something on the
path ... no, it was in the mangroves ... and I ... Gordo wasn't
there ...'*

*The dream dissolved and Miranda sat up. The lights were
on in the room and the curtains were drawn.*

*'Are you back from your dive?' she asked idiotically. And
then, 'But what time is it?'*

*'Dinner time. That's why I woke you. The buffet opens in
twenty minutes and I'm starving. If you want to have a shower,
the bathroom's free.'*

'I must have slept for hours.' She tried to gather herself together.

'Oh, you were out cold. I left you to it. I think you've just caught up on last night.'

'Yes. Except now I won't be able to sleep tonight either. The boat was back late, wasn't it? Did something happen?'

'No. Nothing. We had a great dive. No mantas yet. But some great sharks.'

'Not great white sharks!'

'Hardly. Not out here. Anyway, they are perfectly safe if properly dived. I've told you.' And indeed he had, as he, Mal and Gordo had made some appalling plan to go cage diving with the great whites in Oz somewhat later in the dive year.

'We were back right on time. I've already showered and changed once, and done a night dive with Patrick.'

'You're joking.'

'I told you, you were spark out. Hurry up and have that shower, I want to get to dinner. I'm starving.'

Here, the writer uses the dialogue to contrast Jim's perception of their holiday (all is normal, there is nothing to worry about) with Miranda's vaguely perceived awareness that something is wrong. It also helps to establish the different characters and the relationship between Jim and Miranda. The question that is left in the readers' minds is: Is something wrong with the place, or is something wrong with Miranda?

From *Everybody Shrugged*:

"Did you all receive your copies of the plan?"

"Yes," said Oscar Gotham.

"Yes," said Vandall.

"I didn't get mine yet, sir," said Hunsucker.

....

"*Crap!*" *said Victor. "I even typed it and ran the copies myself, to keep it confidential, and I hand-carried it to your office.*"

"*Then I'm sure it's there, but since my secretary only comes on Tuesdays, she probably hasn't gotten to it yet. If you like, I could go look for it. No, wait, the door is locked.*"

"*Never mind. I was planning to read it aloud anyway. It's just that I was sort of proud of the way it turned out.*"

"*It was excellent,*" *said Oscar, "although there are one or two little things I might have expressed differently.*"

"*Yes, it was quite good,*" *said Vandall.*

"*Thank you, gentlemen, thank you. Now, let's go through it. Atlee, why don't you look on with Homer there?*"

"*No need,*" *said Vandall. "I've committed it to memory.*" *He took the plan out of his breast pocket and shoved it across the table to Hunsucker.*

"*It's got coffee stains on it, Homer.*"

"*I wouldn't complain. That's a luxury we're not going to have much longer. Or these cigars either.*"

This extract is from the prologue of *Everybody Shrugged*.

This scene, which is largely dialogue, sets both the tone and the topic for the whole book, signalling it as a military romp that will be peopled by characters who take themselves and their missions far too seriously. The paranoia of the door timed to remain locked for the whole of the time scheduled for this top-secret Pentagon meeting spirals into farce as latecomers are locked out. Key traits for several of the characters are established using dialogue. Victor's obsessive attention to detail shines through the efforts he has made to be sure everyone had a copy of his document. Vandall also comes across as obsessive – he has already committed the document to memory – and also hypercritical. Where Victor is 'proud' of it and Oscar deems it 'excellent', Vandall damns with faint praise, saying it is 'quite good'.

Dialogue can make or break a novel. If you establish that a character speaks in a particular way, it can be used throughout to show who the speaker is, without ever having to spell it out. Dialogue can show personality, temperament and disposition; it can be used to build or release tension; it can move the plot along; it can hint at hidden agendas, reveal secrets to the reader that the characters themselves don't know. While the readers are engrossed in 'listening' to the characters talk to each other, they will be swept along never noticing that the dialogue is actually designed to speak directly to them.

Milking the action and emotion

Dramatic moments, whether part of rising-tension or releasing-tension scenes, are one of the most powerful constructs of fiction – these are the images that stay in the readers' heads, the moments that have their hearts racing. Don't waste them. Above all, don't summarise them. Milk them for all they've got. Sometimes all it takes is the addition of a few words, or a bit of restructuring.

There is a scene in *The Last Room* where Dariusz realises that the person behind him has a knife. The prose could simply have said, *The person behind him was carrying a knife.*

But the finished version racks up the tension by taking us step by step through Dariusz's realisation.

In his peripheral vision, in the shadows, something gleamed.
A knife. The person behind him was carrying a knife.

Because a dramatic moment can make your book stick in readers' minds, it's always worth getting the most out of it. Dramatic moments often happen quickly. They can be described in few words e.g.

- *Jo teetered at the cliff edge for a couple of seconds before regaining his balance.*
- *Maisie suddenly realised who it was and flung herself into his arms.*
- *The car pulled out in front of him without any warning and Horace drove into the side of it.*

But when writing a dramatic moment into your fiction, remember that for Jo, Maisie or Horace these are not split-second events. Time will slow. Seconds will crawl by. They will experience a whole range of emotions and feelings – terror, shock, amazement, disbelief, relief. They will even be analysing the situation as it happens and might be aware of the faces of other people nearby (frozen in shock perhaps).

This is true also for those who witness moments of high drama such as sudden car crashes. They too run the gamut of emotion as the events unfold. This happens because the brain works at lightning speed, way faster than physical reactions, its emergency response mechanism laying down many more detailed memories. If you've ever been driving and had someone pull out in front of you, giving you maybe a third of a second before the impact, you will know the reality of 'thinking distance' – an absolute awareness of what is happening whilst your body simply cannot react.

And if you can get right inside the head of the character to whom the dramatic event is happening, you will write some compelling prose.

You can employ techniques of language and structure (see the Advanced Techniques sections of earlier chapters) to give realism. You must take care not to overdo the internal analysis. You don't want the reader suddenly to think, wait a minute, this guy must have been balancing on that cliff edge for half an hour!

If you have a viewpoint character in a bit of a sticky situation that is going to lead up to a big dramatic moment, stay with that character's actions, feelings and emotions every step of the way almost second by second. But when you get to the real drama – the event that in reality will be over in seconds – get in even tighter. Go millisecond by millisecond with your character and make the reader experience the event as though it is happening to them.

You will be surprised at how a single sentence such as 'The car pulled out in front of him without any warning and Horace drove into the side of it', can turn into several paragraphs or even pages of compelling prose.

A well-written moment of tension is usually longer than a simple statement of the facts. The trick is in rewording that simple statement in a way that brings the prose to life. A master of milking the dramatic moment was James Herriot. The following example is from *If Only They Could Talk.*

In one of the scenes, Herriot and his boss, Siegfried Farnon, arrive at a farm to carry out a post-mortem. In Herriot's original draft of this, the scene opened:

When he arrived at the house he found that he had forgotten to take his PM knife and decided that he would have to borrow a carving knife.

In the published version, this is how the scene begins:

We arrived at the farmhouse with a screaming of brakes. Siegfried had left his seat and was rummaging about in the boot before the car had stopped shuddering. 'Hell!' he shouted, 'no post mortem knife! Never mind, I'll borrow something from the house.' He slammed down the lid and bustled over to the door.

The draft is a simple statement of events. The final version has speed, urgency and brings the volatile Siegfried centre stage perfectly setting the scene for him to burst into the farmhouse kitchen demanding a really sharp knife from the terrified woman inside. They have of course arrived at the wrong farm.

Specific uses for the toolkits

There are certain circumstances where the toolkits are invaluable:

When it's hard to get started on a scene because it isn't clear how it should best be written.

List the elements. Does the scene build to a climax or is it a reflective scene where a character faces a dilemma i.e. is it a rising-tension or releasing-tension scene? Sometimes it's as simple as working out that a scene is building to a particularly dramatic line that marks it out as a rising-tension scene. Then it's easy, write out all the elements and you have the raw materials to turn it into matchless prose.

When a scene that should be high drama seems to sag.

List out the components in the rising-tension scene toolkit and see if there's anything out of place. A short sentence in flashback perhaps, or a summary of part of the action? Repair those and the scene will lift.

When a reflective scene just seems to be boring and to drag on too long.

Again list out the components in the releasing-tension scene toolkit and see what you have. Did you show when you should have used tell? Have you used real-time when it would have been better to summarize? Rewrite these elements and watch the scene take flight.

When it's hard to get started on a scene because it's just one of those days.

You could cry Writer's Block and take the day off, but hey, isn't that cheating? Does writer's block actually mean anything more than that you've hit a day or a time when you'd rather be doing something else, when it all seems too much effort? And doesn't everyone hit these days in any job? Does the plumber ring you and say s/he can't get round to mend your washing machine today because of Plumber's Block? S/he too probably wants to be out enjoying the sunshine or off to the cinema, anywhere in fact but in your utility room crammed behind your washer, but that's the world we live in.

If you can't find any enthusiasm, get out your toolkits. Write down the elements of the scene if you can't tackle the scene itself. You'll be surprised how it can help. And what if you end up with a whole novel written only in toolkits? Fine. That's a great outline from which to start writing your masterpiece.

These toolkits are not rules of writing. They show the generic elements of the 'usual' form of a work of commercial fiction. That is not the same as suggesting that all commercial fiction sticks to these norms. Of course it doesn't, but the writer who understands the underlying structures will be far more effective in both using them and breaking free of them.

- **Do we use the toolkits and techniques in our own work?** Yes, we do.
- **Do we write every scene by constructing the toolkit outline first?** No, we don't. Sometimes we just write without a thought to structure because the story is in our heads.
- **Do we stick to the toolkit 'rules' i.e. where to show, where to tell, where to use flashback, where to avoid it etc?** On the whole, yes, but we often break these 'rules'. Knowing what the structures are and why they are there makes it easier to recognise when it's a good idea to stray from them.
- **Is it possible to write a whole book following the toolkits?** Yes, it is, and it's quite a neat way to build a first draft.

Rules of writing

Are there any real rules of writing? Possibly just four:

1. **Take responsibility**: only you can make it happen. Sure, some people get lucky and some don't, but you'll get nowhere railing against fate because you don't get the breaks. Be positive. It's your life. It's up to you to make it happen.

2. **Give yourself the best possible chance**: Learn the craft. Learn structure, viewpoint, characterization, markets, everything. Don't fight the fight with one hand tied behind your back.

3. **Be proactive, not reactive**: If you're serious about writing, make room for it. Make writing a part of your life. If you wait for time to become available, it won't. Watch out for how you prioritize.

4. **Learn to put words on paper**. Learn to sit and write without stopping if only for a couple of minutes at a time. It might not be the way you will construct your finished work, but getting words on paper is hard so teach yourself how to do it.

When is a manuscript finished?

Did you know that Tolkien almost didn't let go of *The Lord of the Rings* because he didn't feel he'd got it quite right? Thankfully he was persuaded or the world would have lost a wonderful book. But of course he was right. It wasn't quite finished. There will always be things that could be better, that could be done differently. And there will always be readers who don't like the book. That's fiction. It's subjective. In the history of the world

113

there is no universally liked work of fiction. You certainly shouldn't try to please everyone because you can't.

Agents and publishers say 'Get it perfect' or (more realistically) 'as close to perfect as you can' before you send it. There's a lot in that. Some things you can do mechanically, like spelling, layout, proofreading for typos, quote marks in the right places etc. But even here, you should be realistic. A typo was found in Darwin's *On the Origin of Species* over 100 years after its first publication. If you think of the scholars who have pored over that book, reading in minute detail, often actively on the lookout for something to criticise, it's amazing that a typo could lurk undetected for so long. But it did. So do make every effort, but don't beat yourself up for misplacing a comma.

The mechanics of a tidy, error-free manuscript are one aspect. Building the story into a compelling read is another, and that is what you do over a long apprenticeship. All 'overnight success' stories happened after a lot of hard work (the occasional ghost-written celebrity memoir excepted). You learn to find your writing voice. But rather than just flounder in the dark, it makes sense to shortcut the route. It's a well-trodden path that many others have been down, and they have left advice, tips, tricks and pointers along the way. This book is a part of that. Take advantage. Rather than diving right in with one hand tied behind your back, learn the craft and give yourself the best possible chance for success.

In this book we have looked at
- how to create a short sharp pitch for your book
- the opening of a work of commercial fiction and how to reel in your readers

- the ebb and flow of building and releasing tension as the novel develops
- the climax and resolution and how to leave a reader feeling satisfied they've had a good read
- techniques for bringing your prose to life.

Happy writing, best of luck with the novel and please drop by and let us know how you get on.

Penny & Danuta
www.pennygrubb.com www.danutareah.com

Bibliography

The following (alphabetical by title) are the novels and films we have used as examples in this book:

- *Alien.* Sci-fi horror film. Ridley Scott, director. 1979.
- *American Psycho.* Bret Easton Ellis. 1991.
- *Beowulf.* Anon. Anglo Saxon.
- *Bleak House.* Charles Dickens. First published 1852/3.
- *Bleak Water.* Danuta Reah. HarperCollins 2003 (Hb); 2004 (Pb); 2011 (ebk).
- *Buffy the Vampire Slayer.* TV series. Created by Joss Whedon. 1997-2003.
- *Buried Deep.* Penny Grubb. Fantastic Books Publishing 2014 (ebk & Pb).
- *Crime and Punishment.* Fyodor Dostoyevsky. First published 1866.
- *Everybody Shrugged.* Walt Pilcher. Fantastic Books Publishing 2018 (ebk & Pb).
- *If Only They Could Talk.* James Herriot. First published Michael Joseph 1970.
- *Life Ruins.* Danuta Reah, forthcoming.
- *Like False Money.* Penny Grubb. Robert Hale Ltd 2010 (Hb & ebk); Acorn Press 2011 (Pb); Fantastic Books Publishing 2018 (reissued ebk).
- *Lolita.* Vladimir Nobokov. First published 1955.
- *Night Angels.* Danuta Reah. HarperCollins 2002, (Hb); 2003 (Pb); 2011 (ebk).

- *No Flies on Frank.* Danuta Reah, in Best British Mysteries IV ed Maxim Jakubowski, 2006 (Pb); 2012 (ebk).
- *On the Origin of Species.* Charles Darwin. First published 1859.
- *Only Darkness.* Danuta Reah. HarperCollins 1999 (Hb); 2000 (Pb); 2012 (ebk).
- *Slaughterhouse 5.* Kurt Vonnegut, Vintage Classics, 1991.
- *Strangers.* Danuta Reah writing as Carla Banks. HarperCollins 2006 (Hb); 2007 (Pb); 2012 (ebk).
- *Syrup Trap City.* Penny Grubb. Fantastic Books Publishing 2017 (ebk & Pb).
- *The Catcher in the Rye.* J D Salinger. First published 1951.
- *The Doll Makers.* Penny Grubb. Robert Hale Ltd 2010 (Hb); Acorn Press 2011 (Pb); Fantastic Books Publishing 2013 (ebk).
- *The Forest of Souls.* Danuta Reah writing as Carla Banks. HarperCollins 2005 (Hb); 2006 (Pb); 2011 (ebk).
- *The Group.* Mary McCarthy Virago Modern Classics (this edition 2009)
- *The Jawbone Gang.* Penny Grubb. Robert Hale Ltd 2011 (Hb); Acorn Press 2011 (Pb); Fantastic Books Publishing 2013 (ebk).
- *The Lord of the Rings.* JRR Tolkien. First published George Allen & Unwin 1954.
- *Till They Dropped.* Sue Knight. Fantastic Books Publishing 2016 (ebk & Pb).
- *Tiger Blood.* Penny Grubb. Fantastic Books Publishing 2016 (ebk & Pb).
- *Trainspotting.* Irvine Welsh. Secker & Warburg 1993.

- *Waiting for Gordo.* Sue Knight. Fantastic Books Publishing 2017 (ebk & Pd).
- *Where There's Smoke.* Penny Grubb. Robert Hale Ltd 2012 (Hb); 2013 (ebk); Fantastic Books Publishing 2013 (Pb); 2018 (reissued ebk).

Other books (alphabetical by title) we have used in writing this one:
- *How to write damn good fiction.* James N Frey. Pan Macmillan; 2002
- *How to Write a Damn Good Novel.* James N Frey. St. Martin's Press; 1987
- *How to Write a Damn Good Novel II.* James N Frey. St. Martin's Press; 1994
  James Frey's books are good on all aspects of what it takes to write good fiction.
- *On Writing.* Stephen King. Scribner; 10th Anniversary edition; 2010
  Advice from a master of commercial fiction.
- *Reading a Writer's Mind.* Linda Acaster. Amazon Digital Services; 2012
  This book analyses short stories and gives useful insights into writing techniques.
- *Style in Fiction.* Geoffrey Leech and Mick Short. Pearson. 2007.
  An academic book that analyses the way certain writers use language to create a range of different effects.
- *Techniques of the best-selling author.* Dwight V Swain. University of Oklahoma Press; 1981.
  This book breaks down the individual elements of the toolkits into even more detail.

If you have enjoyed this book and found it useful, please consider leaving a review for Penny and Danuta to let them know what you thought of their work.

Penny and Danuta conduct writers' workshops on many aspects of writing: general fiction, genre fiction, non-fiction for magazines and newspapers, academic writing. If you are interested in writing workshops, please contact Fantastic Books Publishing via the Fantastic Books Store on the link below.

You can find out more about Penny and Danuta on their author pages on the Fantastic Books Store. While you're there, why not browse the rest of our literary offering?

www.FantasticBooksStore.com

www.ingramcontent.com/pod-product-compliance
Lightning Source LLC
Chambersburg PA
CBHW060504280326
41933CB00014B/2862